THE NEW PHILIPPINES

DON LAWSON

THE NEW PHILIPPINES

FRANKLIN WATTS 1986
AN IMPACT BOOK SECOND EDITION
NEW YORK LONDON TORONTO SYDNEY

Originally published as *Marcos and the Philippines*

Map by Vantage Art, Inc.

Photographs courtesy of: AP/Wide World: pp. 12, 16, 22, 25, 75, 84; UPI/Bettmann Newsphotos: pp. 15, 19, 24, 29, 30, 32, 33, 35, 38, 53, 71, 72, 82, 85, 87, 94, 101, 102, 104, 110; Philippine Ministry of Tourism: pp. 43, 45, 46, 47, 48, 54, 57, 59, 115; National Media Production Center/Philippine Ministry of Tourism: p. 66.

Library of Congress Cataloging in Publication Data

Lawson, Don.
The new Philippines.

Rev. ed. of: Marcos and the Philippines. 1984.
Bibliography: p.
Includes index.
Summary: Presents the politics, economics, and modern history of the Philippines, with emphasis on the period from the ascension of Ferdinand Marcos to the installment of Corazon Aquino as new president.
1. Philippines—Politics and government—1946– Juvenile literature. 2. Philippines—Politics and government—Juvenile literature. [1. Philippines—Politics and government] I. Lawson, Don. Marcos and the Philippines. II. Title.
DS686.5.L3 1986 959.9′04 86-15733
ISBN 0-531-10269-6

Printed in the United States of America
5 4 3 2 1

TO ESTELLE MURPHY,
RESPECTED RESEARCHER
AND CO-WORKER IN THE
EDITORIAL VINEYARD

CONTENTS

THE NEW PHILIPPINES

1

CORAZON AQUINO—NEW PRESIDENT OF THE PHILIPPINES

"The long agony is over. We are finally free, and we can be truly proud of the unprecedented way we achieved our freedom—with courage and determination and, most important, in peace."

With those words Corazon Aquino took charge of the Philippine government in a predawn telecast on the morning of February 26, 1986. Only hours before, Ferdinand Marcos, the country's president for the past twenty years, had fled into exile aboard a U.S. Air Force jet.

Now it was up to the fifty-three-year-old "Cory" Aquino to bring some sort of order out of the political chaos that had engulfed the nation for the past several months. Aquino also faced the task of trying to fulfill the hopes of the millions of Filipino people who had brought her to power in what had been a remarkably nonviolent revolution.

The way ahead for the politically inexperienced Aquino threatened to be a difficult one. But her tremendous popular support and the international expression of good will toward her and her new regime gave strong promise of a bright new future for the troubled Republic of the Philippines.

Corazon Aquino takes the oath of office as president of the Philippines on February 25, 1986, succeeding Ferdinand Marcos. Administering the oath is Claudio Teehankee, an associate justice of the Supreme Court. In the center of the picture is Doña Aurora Aquino, mother of Corazon Aquino's slain husband, Benigno Aquino.

HOW AQUINO CAME TO POWER

The Assassination of Benigno Aquino

Although it was not apparent at the time, Corazon Aquino's rise to power actually began with the assassination of her husband, Benigno Aquino, in late August 1983. Benigno Aquino, or "Ninoy," as he had affectionately been called, was a Filipino senator who had strongly opposed Ferdinand Marcos' military dictatorship of the Philippines. So troublesome had Aquino's political opposition become that Marcos had him thrown into jail. He was released from jail only when he and his wife and family agreed to go into exile in the United States.

While the Aquinos were in the United States, opposition to Marcos' dictatorial rule continued to grow in the Philippines. At the time of Aquino's exile, Marcos had been president of the Philippines for eighteen years, even though the Republic's original constitution said that no president could serve for more than two consecutive four-year terms. In 1972 Marcos had proclaimed a new constitution with himself as president and prime minister (the constitution was adopted in 1973). Soon after, he imposed martial law throughout the country. This meant the end of civil authority, with the military taking over all law-enforcement responsibilities.

By the early 1980s, as a result of political pressure, Marcos had lifted the restrictions of martial law and promised to hold free parliamentary elections in "the near future." Marcos himself was not up for reelection, but it was rumored that he was in poor health and that he might step down.

At this point Benigno Aquino decided that the time was ripe for a return to his homeland. He planned to resume his political opposition to Marcos, take part in the elections, now scheduled for 1984, and organize the democratic opposition. He also said he intended to try to negotiate with Marcos for a return to constitutional democracy.

Aquino's wife, his brother, and even political allies tried to stop the exiled senator from returning. President Marcos told Aquino he could not be held responsible for what might happen if Aquino did return. But Aquino ignored all this. He arrived back in the Philippines on August 21, 1983, aboard a commercial jumbo jet. His wife and family remained in the United States. Soon after the plane landed at the Manila airport it was boarded by an armed military escort. Exactly what happened in the next few moments instantly became the subject of wide controversy.

What is definitely known is that just seconds after Aquino walked down the steps from the plane, accompanied by his escort, he was shot through the head and died almost at once. Moments later a whole volley of shots rang out, and another man lay dead on the tarmac, or runway. This man was later identified as Rolando Galman. Galman, authorities claimed, had murdered Aquino and was in turn gunned down by Aquino's military escort.

But civilian eyewitnesses to the twin killings claimed instead that Aquino had been shot by one of his escorts who was on the ramp behind him. They also said that after Aquino was shot, the already lifeless body of Galman had been pushed out the back door of a van onto the tarmac and that one of Aquino's escorts had then emptied his carbine into the body of the dead "assassin."

When Corazon Aquino received word of her husband's murder, she immediately accused President Marcos of arranging it. In the Philippines, Aquino's political followers blamed both Marcos and his overzealous top military command. There was also violent public reaction to Aquino's assassination. "Ninoy" had been a greatly loved figure among all freedom-loving Filipinos. The rumors that he had been gunned down on orders of his

Congressman Stephen Solarz (Dem.-NY) and his wife (crying) view the body of Benigno Aquino. Next to Mrs. Solarz is Salvador Laurel, eventually to become the Philippines' new vice president.

Angry mobs demonstrate in the streets of the Philippines, to protest the murder of the much-loved Benigno Aquino.

chief political rival, Ferdinand Marcos, caused riots to erupt throughout the Philippines.

Marcos Appoints an Investigating Committee

To restore order in the land, Marcos announced that he would appoint an "impartial" committee to investigate the slaying. It soon became apparent, however, that Marcos had loaded the committee with his own supporters and henchmen, and it was disbanded. Marcos then promised that a new and "truly impartial" investigative panel would be named in the near future. Opposition leaders quickly rejected the idea that any government panel would be able to reach an objective, unbiased conclusion.

By this time Corazon Aquino had returned to the Philippines, and she stated publicly, "The whole trouble is that Marcos is the first suspect. As long as Marcos is in power, there can be no fair and independent investigation."

Meanwhile, pressure for an honest disclosure of the facts surrounding the assassination was being brought to bear on Marcos by the United States. Although the Philippines is an independent republic, it still has strong historic, military, and economic ties with the United States. Through the U.S. State Department and his personal emissaries, President Ronald Reagan made it clear to Marcos that continued American support of the Philippines could well depend on a quick resolution of the Aquino situation.

There then followed a series of investigations by successive committees, none of which seemed to result in any satisfactory answers. Impartial observers pointed out that Marcos was merely stalling for time, hoping that the Aquino problem would simply go away. This was a tactic Marcos had often used successfully in the past to stifle political opposition. But it failed to work this time.

Finally, in 1984, a special judicial panel headed by Justice Corazon Agrava ruled that military personnel were probably responsible for Benigno Aquino's assassination. The panel ordered that General Fabian Ver, chief of staff of the Philippine army, and a number of Ver's top aides be tried for the murder.

The trial lasted for ten months, extending well into 1985. Meanwhile, political opposition to the Marcos regime continued to mount. Many opposition rallies were led by Corazon Aquino, who suddenly found herself a heroine among the Filipino masses.

Confident of a favorable outcome, Marcos decided to directly challenge his opponents. On November 3, 1985, Marcos announced on American television that an election would be held early in 1986 in which he himself would stand for re-election. There was no doubt that the Philippine president fully expected his mandate from the people to be renewed in this "snap" election.

On December 2, 1985, General Ver and twenty-six of his accused co-conspirators were acquitted of Benigno Aquino's murder. The next day Corazon Aquino announced her own candidacy for the presidency. The election was scheduled for February 7, 1986.

The Campaign

When Cory Aquino returned to the Philippines following her husband's death, few Filipinos knew much about her. Born January 25, 1933, she was the sixth of eight children in the Cojuangco family. The Cojuangcos were wealthy sugar and coconut plantation owners from Tarlac, a province just 65 miles (104 km) northwest of Manila. After attending schools in Manila, Cory Cojuangco was sent to the United States where she earned degrees in French and mathematics at Mount St. Vincent College in New York City. She then returned to Manila, where she enrolled in law school. But in 1956, while still in school, she abandoned her law studies to marry Ninoy Aquino, the twenty-two-year-old mayor of Concepcion. Ninoy was the youngest mayor in the Philippines.

As her husband's political career prospered, and he advanced from mayor to governor and finally to senator, Cory Aquino remained quietly in the background. Although she strongly supported her husband's opposition

Armed forces chief General Fabian Ver stands trial, with twenty-five other soldiers and civilians, for plotting the assassination of Benigno Aquino. He and the others were acquitted, in spite of the strong evidence linking them with the murder.

to Marcos, Cory concentrated on being a good wife and rearing their five children.

But the Aquinos' quiet middle-class life was suddenly disrupted in 1972 when Ninoy was jailed for his continued public criticism of President Marcos. Released in 1980 for medical reasons—he had heart trouble—Ninoy and his family were exiled. They moved to Boston, where they remained until his fateful return to the Philippines in 1983.

Almost in spite of herself Cory Aquino was pushed to the forefront of the anti-Marcos movement that had gained momentum in the aftermath of the assassination. Though she did try to rally the followers of this opposition movement, she insisted that she had no interest in political office. Nevertheless, more than a million Filipinos signed petitions calling on her to run for the presidency. These petitions, and the acquittal of the army officers accused of killing her husband, convinced Cory that she should seek political office.

If Marcos were to be defeated, it was generally agreed that all of the opposition forces would have to unite behind one candidate. A split opposition would divide the votes between Aquino and any other opposition candidate and probably give Marcos the election. The hope for unity was temporarily dashed when a former senator, Salvador "Doy" Laurel, fifty-seven, announced that he, too, would run as an opposition candidate for the presidency against Marcos.

A longtime Marcos foe, Laurel headed a party called the United Nationalist Democratic Organization (UNIDO). Laurel had earlier agreed that he would run as a vice-presidential candidate on the Aquino-for-president ticket but only if Aquino agreed to run under the UNIDO banner. When Aquino refused to do this, Laurel called off the single ticket arrangement and announced: "I can sacrifice myself. I can sacrifice the presidency. But I cannot sacrifice my party, my principles, and the people who have worked so hard all these years to put up the political machine that can topple the Marcos dictatorship."

Cory Aquino responded by saying she would pursue her own campaign, with or without Laurel.

The Aquino party adopted "Laban" as its name. Meaning "fight," Laban was a coalition of anti-Marcos groups. The "L" handsign, made by extending the thumb and forefinger, soon became the symbol of the Laban party. The color yellow was adopted as the party's color, symbolizing a bright and promising new future for the Philippines. Despite the obvious popularity of Laban and Aquino, however, impartial observers doubted that Marcos could be defeated unless Aquino and Laurel joined forces.

At this point Jaime Cardinal Sin, leader of the Roman Catholic Church in the Philippines, entered the picture. A devout Roman Catholic, Corazon Aquino had frequently turned to Cardinal Sin for advice during the trying times following her husband's death. The cardinal helped persuade her to run for the presidency, and now he persuaded her to unite with Salvador Laurel, who would be vice president, under the UNIDO banner. Their last-minute decision to form an alliance—only an hour before the legal midnight filing deadline—caused wide celebration throughout the Philippines.

But wily politician Ferdinand Marcos was not going to be easy to defeat. For one thing he and his party, the New Society Movement (KBL), had a campaign fund of $160 million, about six times the amount that Aquino and Laurel had at their disposal. In addition, Marcos and his supporters controlled the nation's newspapers and radio and television stations, which allowed almost no media coverage of the Aquino campaign. The KBL also controlled most of the provincial governorships and mayoral offices.

Marcos' first move was a tried-and-true political boss's gesture—he immediately began to disperse vast sums of money by way of political patronage. This money included pay increases of $15 million to the military forces, $62 million in Christmas bonuses to more than a million civilian government employees, a $25 million series of interest-free loans to sugar marketing companies, and a sharp decrease in interest on loans to sugar planters. In rural areas he reduced the cost of electricity and began a program to increase electrification of towns and villages.

Cardinal Jaime Sin, the Archbishop of Manila, was a strong supporter of Corazon Aquino's candidacy and showed little hesitation about mixing his politics and religion.

Such "pork barrel" expenditures were intended as a realistic reminder to many voters that for their own good they had better remain loyal to Marcos.

But there was very little that the Marcos forces could do to stem the growing popularity of Corazon Aquino. In fact, the steady yet forceful Aquino seemed to have become something of a folk heroine almost overnight. Wherever she went vast crowds gathered, sometimes even standing in the rain for hours awaiting her arrival. When she finally did arrive her admirers chanted, "Cory! Cory! Cory!" for many minutes before permitting her to speak.

Candidate Aquino's message was a simple one. If elected, she would end the Marcos dictatorship and return true democracy to the Philippines. She would empty the jails of political prisoners, break up the sugar and coconut monopolies, lower taxes, and increase employment. What she was saying was not especially new, but her apparent sincerity and moral indignation at the obvious plundering of the Philippine economy by the corrupt Marcos regime soon turned the Aquino campaign into a political crusade.

Marcos, too, promised reform. In addition, he named as his vice-presidential running mate seventy-five-year-old Arturo Tolentino. This was a politically astute move for two reasons. First, Tolentino was a longtime critic of Marcos who had earlier been fired as the country's foreign minister for his opposition to the president's views. Marcos' selection of Tolentino as his running mate was meant to prove to the public that Marcos was truly interested in reform. Secondly, the selection of Tolentino ended many Filipinos' fears that Imelda Marcos, the president's wife, might succeed him in office. Many observers had said that as soon as he was reelected the physically ailing Marcos would make Imelda vice president and then step aside and let his wife succeed to the presidency. Most Filipinos, even Marcos supporters, did not want the unpredictable and financially irresponsible Imelda running the government. Marcos had long insisted that he had no intention of making such a move, and Imelda had said she did not seek high political office, but many did not

Ferdinand Marcos and Arturo Tolentino campaign in the northern Philippines during the 1986 elections.

Corazon Aquino and Salvador Laurel campaign in Cebu, the second largest city in the Philippines.

believe her. Now, with the selection of Tolentino, the Imelda rumors were at least temporarily silenced.

Marcos also made every effort to quiet the persistent rumors about his ailing health. Although he denied the stories, it was reliably reported that he suffered from a rare disease (*systemic lupus erythematosus*) that had damaged his kidneys so badly that he had already had a kidney transplant and frequently had to undergo kidney dialysis.

Now, as he campaigned both in public and on national television, Marcos tried to disprove the rumors about his poor health. He also tried to prove his sincerity about reforming the country both politically and economically. To many observers Marcos' appeals, which frequently referred to his own and his country's past glories, fell flat. The frail, puffy-faced dictator who now appeared before them was a caricature of the youthful reformer and World War II hero who had first appeared on the Philippine political scene as a member of the House of Representatives in 1949. Despite Marcos' all-out campaign in late 1985 and early 1986, it soon became clear that if he were to be re-elected it would have to be his political machine that would carry him to victory.

And the Marcos political machine almost did just that.

The Election

One of the greatest fears of both Aquino followers and U.S. government officials was that the election might be rigged and stolen by the Marcos machine. If this happened, there was every danger that a bloody, full-scale revolution could break out. The first of these fears was realized. The election was indeed rigged. The second fear was only partially realized. A revolution did follow, but it was a virtually bloodless one.

Before the election, Marcos tried to reassure everyone that it would be conducted fairly, and he invited a delegation of official U.S. observers to be on the scene to witness election procedures. This twenty-member delegation, appointed by President Reagan, was headed by Senate Foreign Relations Committee Chairman Richard

Lugar. In addition, a volunteer Filipino organization known as the National Citizens Movement for Free Elections (NAMFREL) also planned to be an election watchdog. But the official vote count was to be taken by the Marcos-dominated Commission on Elections (COMELEC).

On election day a surprising number of Filipino voters, some 24 million, went to the polls. This large turnout was based on a love for democracy, the strong reaction of "people power" to which challenger Aquino had appealed, and the fact that for the first time in sixteen years the voters were being allowed to "freely" elect a president. Many voters walked to the 90,000 polling places throughout the Philippines. Others came by horse- or oxen-drawn wagons. Some even came by boat. But come they did.

The polls had not long been closed on the evening of February 7, however, when reports began to filter into Manila from throughout the islands of widespread election fraud—intimidation of voters through threats of physical violence, vote buying, the actual stealing of ballot boxes, and so on. Many members of NAMFREL valiantly attempted to prevent the theft of ballots by physically defending the sealed ballot boxes. This resulted in several deaths.

Senator Richard Lugar almost immediately reported that "a very disturbing pattern of incidents has emerged. The vote count is being shaped to what President Marcos needs." In at least one province all of the votes were for Marcos and none for Aquino. Marcos endeavored to explain this by saying that particular province was largely populated by members of the Marcos family.

Less than a day after the polls closed Marcos announced that he was the winner. He had defeated Aquino, he said, by some 13 million votes to 11 million. The official vote count, Marcos said, would be available to the world within a few days.

But Corazon Aquino also declared that she was the winner.

In Washington government officials said they would delay any formal U.S. response to the election for several days.

The following few days proved to be dramatic ones. As charges and countercharges of fraud flew back and forth in the Philippines it soon became evident that even if Marcos did succeed in continuing as president it was doubtful that he could successfully govern the badly divided electorate without the use of military force. Aquino and her followers publicly vowed to go on protesting Marcos' rule.

When the Philippines' National Assembly formally declared that Marcos had been reelected, Aquino followers staged a 13-mile-long (21-km) protest parade in the streets of Manila. Throughout the islands there were similar demonstrations. A Catholic Bishops' Conference of the Philippines went on record claiming that Marcos had stolen the election. Since 80 percent of the Filipinos are Catholics, this declaration had a powerful effect. At one rally Aquino announced a "People's Victory" campaign, which was to include nonviolent boycotts in the coming weeks as well as a nationwide general strike.

This situation, of course, was exactly what the U.S. government had feared, and some members of Congress began to call for Marcos to step down. President Reagan tried to bring some sort of order out of the Philippines chaos by sending veteran negotiator Philip Habib to Manila to try to reconcile Marcos and Aquino. Reagan eventually issued a statement saying that "the election's credibility was called into question, both within the Philippines and in the U.S." This statement was a severe blow to Marcos. Earlier, Reagan had seemed less outraged at the apparent rigging of the election and had even said that there was a possibility that "fraud was occurring on both sides." Now, however, the Reagan administration had apparently made up its mind on which side of the political fence it planned to come down.

The Rebellion

Meanwhile, Marcos and Aquino further complicated matters by each having themselves sworn in as the new president of the Philippines. A House of Representatives

A policeman escorts a suspected ballot box thief back to a polling station in Mandaluyong. There were many such incidents of foul play in the 1986 elections, despite Marcos' promise to run a clean election.

Marcos' Defense Minister Juan Ponce Enrile (right) and Deputy Armed Forces Chief Lieutenant General Fidel Ramos announce at a news conference that they no longer support the Marcos government. Both men later obtained similar jobs in the Aquino government.

Foreign Affairs subcommittee voted unanimously to temporarily cut off U.S. aid to the Philippine government.

As the pressures continued to mount, Marcos began to issue veiled threats that he would call out the Filipino army to put down the Aquino-sponsored demonstrations. But Marcos no longer had full control of the nation's military forces. On February 22, Defense Minister Juan Ponce Enrile and Military Vice Chief of Staff Lieutenant General Fidel Ramos seized control of the nation's military headquarters and demanded that Marcos resign.

The next day Marcos deployed armored combat units against the rebels Enrile and Ramos and their defecting aides and threatened to destroy them and the military headquarters. But thousands of unarmed demonstrators moved in to form a solid wall and block the path of the armored units. Marcos did not give the final order for the tanks to move forward against this blockade of defenseless bodies. If he had—and if the order had been obeyed—hundreds of demonstrators would certainly have died beneath the tank treads. Later Marcos said he would never have given a command that meant the killing of civilians.

Rumors soon began to circulate that Marcos and his wife and aides were planning to flee or had already fled the country. To quell these rumors Marcos appeared on television, vowing to defend his twenty-year rule against the rebellion.

On February 24, Enrile and Ramos declared a new provisional government of the Philippines, to be headed by Corazon Aquino. Marcos, in turn, again went on television to call upon his supporters to gather at the presidential palace to defend him. This time, however, his appearance was suddenly interrupted when Aquino followers took over the central TV station and cut the telecast from the air.

During all of this tense period there was little doubt that behind the scenes strings were being pulled in Washington to keep the revolution as bloodless as possible and to help Marcos escape into exile if he so desired. After

Opposite: *priests and nuns pray as they use their unarmed bodies to block tanks heading toward the building where the rebel military leaders are camped out.* Above: *Marcos and his family go on TV to reassure the nation that they are still in charge of the government. In a later, similar broadcast, Marcos' TV announcement was cut short, as opposition groups took over the TV station.*

Marcos did flee it was revealed that Senator Paul Laxalt of Nevada played a key role in getting Marcos to leave.

Laxalt was a longtime friend of Marcos who had earned his trust over the years. When Marcos could get no commitment of continued support from the Reagan administration, he spoke by telephone to Laxalt in a White House office.

"Senator, what do you think?" Laxalt said Marcos asked him. "Should I step down?"

"I am not bound by diplomatic restraints," Laxalt replied. "I am talking only for myself. I think you should cut and cut clean. The time has come." There was a long silence before Marcos finally said, "I am so very disappointed." Marcos, of course, could have had no doubt that Laxalt was speaking for all of Congress and the Reagan administration, which had clearly decided to give up on the Marcos regime.

Within a matter of hours after Marcos' conversation with Senator Laxalt, the American ambassador to the Philippines, Stephen Bosworth, made arrangements with the U.S. Air Force for the next important step. Four helicopters were provided to ferry Marcos, his wife Imelda, Army Chief of Staff Fabian Ver, and a large party of aides from Manila to Clark Air Force Base. Nine hours later the entourage of exiles was flown by U.S. Air Force jet to the island of Guam. There they remained for only a short time before being flown by U.S. Air Force jet to Hawaii, where it was rumored Marcos might make his permanent home in exile.

On February 26, 1986, President Corazon Aquino's government was publicly recognized by President Reagan and the United States as the official government of the Republic of the Philippines.

A battered Marcos finally flees the country. Here he is seen being helped from a U.S. aircraft by Air Force personnel after arriving at Honolulu's Hickam Air Force Base.

THE IMPORTANCE OF THE PHILIPPINES TO THE UNITED STATES

The Philippines is one of America's most important strategic military outposts in the Pacific. This is why the United States wants a stable government there whose president is an American ally.

The United States is also important to the Philippines. The United States had long helped keep Marcos in power by providing vast sums of money to bolster the Philippines' sagging economy. There was little doubt that the United States was ready to continue this aid to the new Aquino government.

There were, however, certain immediate problems. For one thing, under Marcos the Philippines had fallen badly into debt—a debt the Aquino government inherited. The Marcos government at the time of its fall owed foreign countries, mainly the United States, more than $26 billion. It was in the interest of both President Aquino and the Reagan administration that this debt be paid back.

If the Philippines were to default on this debt, that is, fail to pay it back, all future economic aid to that country might very well stop. On its part the United States would not only lose all the money loaned, but the Philippines might also take over the two U.S. military bases there and even lease them to somebody else—perhaps the Soviet Union.

Corazon Aquino has said publicly that she wants these American bases out of the Philippines, and there are many Filipinos who agree with her. But their presence adds vast sums of money annually to the Republic's treasury, and it is doubtful that the new president would make any immediate drastic moves to further damage her nation's ailing economy. In fact, the U.S. leases on the bases do not run out until 1991, and President Aquino now says she plans "to keep her options open" until then before deciding what to do about their eventual fate. Most likely, the Philippines and the United States will work out some mutually agreeable new arrangement regarding the bases—unless the Aquino government falters. If at any time it begins to look like the communists could take over, the United States would have to seriously consider taking military action to preserve the Philippines as the key Pacific bastion that it has been since the turn of the twentieth century.

The Two U.S. Military Bases

The two U.S. military installations that are so important to both the Philippines and the United States are the Subic Bay Naval Base and Clark Air Force Base, two of the largest American bases outside the United States. Together these bases are occupied by more than 16,000 service personnel and provide major support for U.S. military activities in both the Pacific and Indian oceans.

In the spring of 1983, the U.S. government renewed an agreement with the Philippines that involves paying "rent" on these bases until 1991 in the amount of $900 million. In addition, the two bases provide jobs paying about $300 million in wages to some 40,000 Filipinos, there are a variety of valuable service contracts, and there is the money spent in the Philippines by U.S. service men and women. Although seemingly costly, this arrangement was regarded by most international experts as an excellent bargain for the United States—in fact a virtual Philippine "giveaway."

The huge naval base at Subic Bay, on the western coast of Luzon Island, and nearby Clark Air Force Base together serve as a military security shield for the United States and its allies in a region that has recently seen an enormous military buildup by the Soviet Union. Together the two bases form a vital defense link from the Philippines, Japan, and Korea to the eastern coast of Australia. Westward, the defense line runs into the Indian Ocean and the Persian Gulf, through which oil supplies vital to the Western world are transported.

Clark Air Force Base, with its 8,700 service men and women is the home of the Thirteenth Air Force and several fighter units of the Pacific Air Force, whose headquarters

Subic Bay Naval Base in the Philippines. The base is a major supply and ship repair facility for the U.S. Seventh Fleet.

are in Hawaii. Clark also provides air support for U.S. naval operations in the Indian Ocean and the Persian Gulf.

The Subic Bay Base, with its 7,500 U.S. personnel, is a major supply and ship repair facility. It provides support for the U.S. Seventh Fleet, whose ships operate throughout the Western Pacific and the Indian Ocean. There is also a naval airfield at Subic Bay which is the land base for the Seventh Fleet's aircraft carrier strike force.

It is estimated that it would cost between $8 billion and $10 billion to relocate these two vital military bases elsewhere in the Pacific. And from a strategic military standpoint, they would not be as ideally situated if located elsewhere—say, on Guam. Ships and planes would have to travel much greater distances at any other location, and there would be other problems, not the least of which would be the loss of the skilled, low-paid Filipino work force.

Growing Soviet Power in Asia

Since the end of the Vietnam War in the early 1970s, the Soviet Union has gradually expanded its military capability in Asia by using Vietnam as a base for its naval and air operations. One of the key Vietnamese installations taken over by the Russians was the former U.S. base at Cam Ranh Bay, which the United States was forced to abandon when it left Vietnam.

Late in 1983, the Soviets deployed offensive bombers at Cam Ranh Bay with a roundtrip range of 3,000 miles (4,800 km). These bombers, called TU16s, or Badgers, are capable of reaching numerous U.S. installations in the region, including those in the Philippines. Also stationed at Cam Ranh Bay by 1986 were Soviet nuclear-powered, nuclear-armed submarines, as well as surface and support ships, that present a clear threat to the United States and its allies throughout the Far East.

Officials at Clark Air Force Base and Subic Bay Naval Base, as well as those at the Pentagon in Washington, regard the Soviet buildup in Vietnam as ominous. They point out, however, that the United States should remain more than an even match for the Russians in Asia as long as it keeps its guard up in the Philippines. But this situation caused heightened concern on the part of the U.S. government during the Marcos-Aquino political crisis.

2

SOME FACTS ABOUT THE PHILIPPINES

The Republic of the Philippines is made up of a long string of some 7,100 mountainous islands in the southwestern Pacific Ocean area off the coast of Southeast Asia. The main group of islands from Luzon in the north to Mindanao in the south is about 1,000 miles (1,600 km) long and 300 miles (480 km) wide. The approximate land area is 115,830 square miles (300,000 sq km). This is roughly the size of Arizona or Illinois and Wisconsin combined. The United States is 6,000 miles (9,600 km) to the northeast.

The population (1984 est. *World Almanac*) was 55,528,000.

The ten major islands are Luzon, Mindanao, Samar, Negros, Palawan, Panay, Mindoro, Leyte, Cebu, and Bohol. They range in size from Luzon, which is 40,420 square miles (105,092 sq km), down to Bohol, which is 1,492 square miles (3,879 sq km). The smallest island among the fewer than twenty that are inhabited is Siquijor, with an area of 129 square miles (335 sq km).

MAJOR CITIES

The capital of the Philippines is Manila, with a 1980 population of 1,626,249. The population of the entire Manila

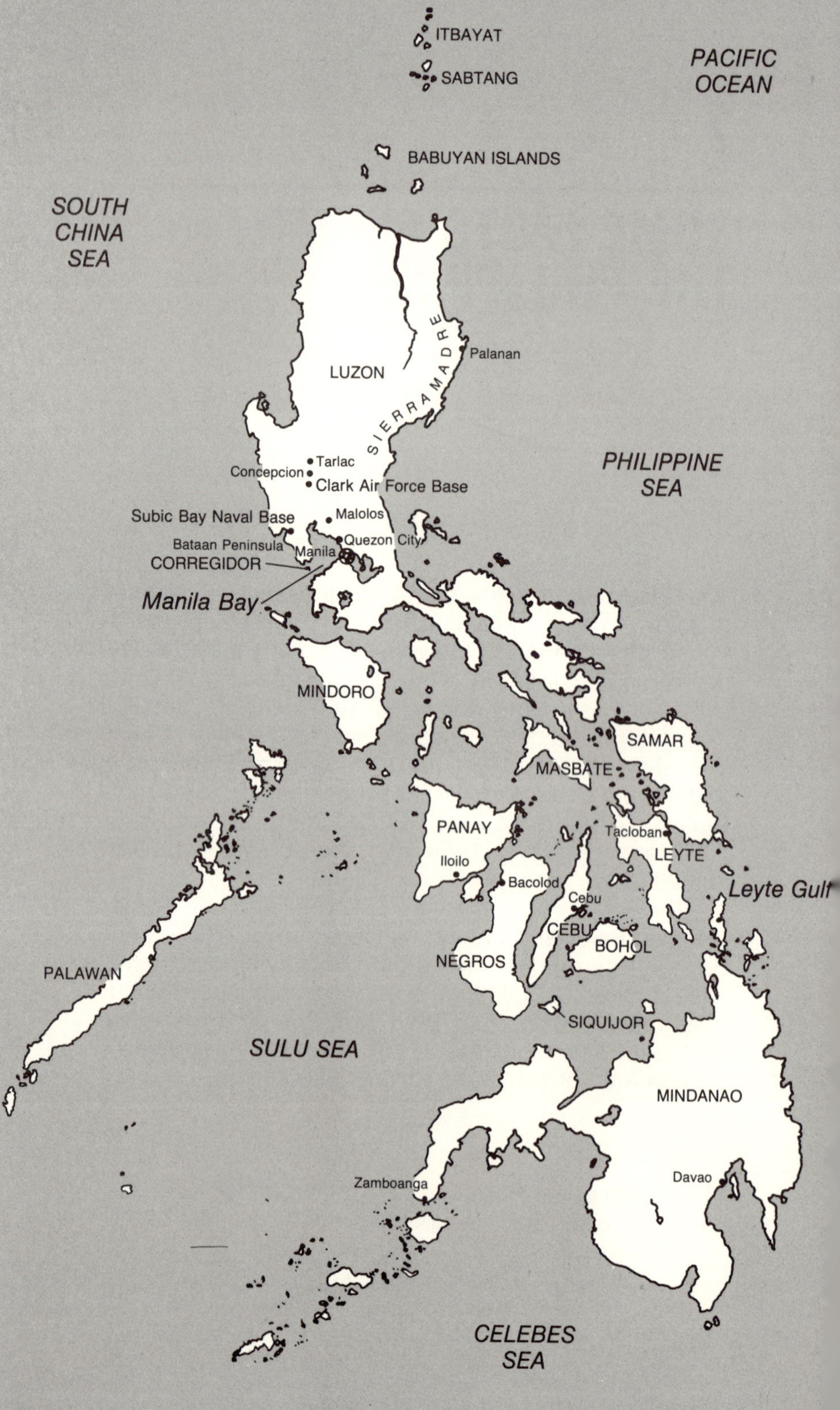
ITBAYAT
SABTANG
PACIFIC OCEAN
BABUYAN ISLANDS
SOUTH CHINA SEA
SIERRA MADRE
Palanan
LUZON
Tarlac
Concepcion
Clark Air Force Base
PHILIPPINE SEA
Subic Bay Naval Base
Malolos
Quezon City
Bataan Peninsula
Manila
CORREGIDOR
Manila Bay
MINDORO
SAMAR
MASBATE
PANAY
Tacloban
LEYTE
Iloilo
Bacolod
Leyte Gulf
Cebu
CEBU
BOHOL
NEGROS
PALAWAN
SIQUIJOR
SULU SEA
MINDANAO
Zamboanga
Davao
CELEBES SEA

A newly developed suburb of Manila

metropolitan area, however, is almost 6 million. The old capital is Quezon City, northeast of Manila, with a population of 1,165,990.

Other important cities and their populations include Davao on Mindanao, 611,311; Zamboanga, also on Mindanao, 334,275; Cebu on Cebu Island, 489,208; Bacolod on Negros, 226,604; Iloilo on Panay, 244,211; and Tarlac on Luzon, 121,400.

CLIMATE AND CROPS

The climate of the Philippines is tropical. Rainfall is generally heavy but seasonal, with most of the rain falling between June and November. Precipitation ranges from 50 to 180 inches (125 to 450 cm) a year, depending on the location. Most of the rain falls in the uplands. The lowlands lie in what is called a "rain shadow," with the upland mountains blocking off the moisture-filled air from the ocean.

The late summer and early autumn months between August and October often bring destructive typhoons to the islands. These fierce storms strike most frequently north of Manila. The Philippines is also subject to violent earthquakes, most of them occurring on Mindanao.

Because of the generally fertile soil found in the lowlands and on the mountain slopes, and the year-round warm-to-moderate temperatures, the Philippines is rich in many agricultural products. These include rice, corn, bananas, citrus fruits, nuts, various root crops, coconuts, tobacco, sisal (hemp), and sugar cane. The Philippines is a world leader in coconut production, and its hemp is the best natural fiber available. During World War II, when Japan occupied the Philippines, the world shortage of hemp caused serious packaging problems, especially in the United States and Great Britain. Today, plastic cord is widely used in place of hemp—even in Filipino fishermen's nets. In the upland areas, vast forests supply timber and other forest products. Philippine mahogany is famous throughout the world.

"Geepneys" such as these are a common sight in Philippine cities. They are used as minibuses to taxi people around.

A mountainside in the Philippines used for cultivating rice paddies. Called rice terraces, these areas are carved by hand from mud and stone. Terraces rise to an altitude of 5,000 feet (1,500 m). If placed end to end, these terraces would encircle the globe.

Making hemp

Bacolod is the "sugar central" of the Philippines, meaning that it is the main sugar-producing district, with vast stretches of sugar plantations.

LANGUAGES AND RELIGION

There are several major languages spoken in the Philippines. Among them are Pilipino, Tagalog, English, and Spanish. Since 1946, Pilipino has been the official language of the Republic. It is based on Tagalog, which is a Malayan dialect. About half the people speak English, and a number of them also speak Spanish. English and Spanish are commonly used for government and commercial purposes. In addition, there are at least seventy-five native languages and dialects spoken throughout the islands.

Religion is a significant factor in the Philippines. At least 80 percent of the population is Roman Catholic, and several million people are Protestant. This makes it the only predominantly Christian nation in Asia. Members of minority religions include Moslems, Buddhists, and others. The fact that the Philippine population is mainly Catholic and that Catholicism is opposed to birth control has resulted in a very high birth rate and severe overpopulation problems in the Philippines.

GOVERNMENT

The United States governed the Philippines from the end of the Spanish-American War in the late 1890s to the end of World War II in the mid-1940s. The Republic gained its independence on July 4, 1946. Since then, the Filipinos have experienced a rocky road to freedom and democracy, one marked by occasional peasant revolutions, riotous demonstrations by students and workers, and despotic one-man rule in the person of its former president, Ferdinand Marcos.

During the latter years of U.S. colonialism in the Philippines, the country was allowed to prepare for independence. It adopted a constitution patterned after the U.S. Constitution and instituted voting reforms.

First adopted in 1935, the original Philippine constitution had two features that distinguished it from the U.S. Constitution. It provided for a single, six-year term for the president, and there was only a single house (unicameral) legislature. In 1940, these features were changed by amendment. In 1946, when independence was declared, further amendments were made. Each of these amendments was aimed at decentralizing the government by decreasing the power of the president and giving more authority directly to the people in the seventy-three provinces.

Under the 1946 constitution, there was a president and vice president, both of whom were to be elected by popular vote to four-year terms. The president was not permitted to serve for more than two consecutive terms.

There was also a two-house legislature, the Senate and House of Representatives. The judicial system was headed by an eleven-member Supreme Court, with the chief justice and the associate justices appointed by the president. A system of lower courts, also similar to that in the United States, was provided for the provinces, municipalities, chartered cities, and *barrios*, or rural villages.

Civil administration in each of the provinces was headed by a governor and two other board members. Municipalities and chartered cities were to have mayor-council governments, and the barrios had limited local control of their own affairs.

Under this constitutional system, the government of the Philippines worked moderately well as a democracy until 1965, when Marcos came to power. Two political parties, the Nationalist and Liberal parties, dominated Philippine politics. Unfortunately, there was little actual difference in their ideas about how to run the government. Filipino voters had a tendency to vote for political leaders with powerful personalities rather than for able administrators. Also unfortunately, both fraud—vote stealing, dishonest vote counting, false voter registrations, etc.—and violence became common in Philippine politics.

Reform movements were started to eliminate political fraud and violence, but third parties have had very little success in Philippine politics. Marcos promised to create his own brand of reform—a common promise made by all potential political dictators—if he were given enough power.

By way of taking all authority into his own hands, Marcos abolished the vice-presidency. He then had himself named both president and prime minister, and the two-term presidential provision was abolished. Technically, this was legal, since it was part of the Marcos constitution adopted in 1973. To further establish his "legal" right to remain in power under this new document, Marcos held a rigged referendum in 1977 in which "no" votes were simply not counted correctly. His earlier declaration of martial law, however, continued to cause unrest, so he formally lifted it in 1981 and gave the legislative assembly limited rights to pass certain legislation. He also released political prisoners—among them Benigno Aquino—and promised to no longer rule by decree. In June of that year, he was reelected president for a six-year term.

Soon after his reelection, however, Marcos resumed his old dictatorial ways. The legislative assembly became a rubber stamp, automatically approving Marcos' demand decrees without debate, and the military once again was called on to enforce the so-called law. Throughout the islands, the judiciary was no longer called on to decide legal disputes, since the military had taken the law into its own hands.

Under Marcos, the Philippines became a democracy in name only. Technically, all male and female citizens of fifteen years of age or older who could read and write were entitled to vote in local, provincial, and national elections. But when those elections, especially at the national level, are either rigged by fraudulent voting or nonexistent, voting becomes an exercise in futility. The fact that Marcos received 88 percent of the vote in the 1981 presidential election was not so much a sign of his popularity as it was an indication that any and all opposition to him was ruthlessly suppressed.

It was this situation that reformer Benigno Aquino hoped to have a hand in changing when he returned to the Philippines. And it was just such reform that Aquino's widow, Corazon, partially succeeded in accomplishing in the election of 1986. Under newly elected President Aquino additional reforms would most certainly follow, including the adoption of a new constitution.

THE FILIPINO WAY OF LIFE

Most Filipinos are of Malaysian descent. A few thousand, perhaps 15,000, are dark-skinned Negritos and are considered to be non-Malaysian. Among the Malaysians there are many ancestral divisions. These range from the Cebuanos and Tagalogs—the two largest divisions—to the Pampangos and Ilongos, which are among the smallest.

Many Filipinos also have Chinese, Hindu, Spanish, and American ancestors. At least a million are part Chinese.

Population growth is a serious problem in the Philippines. In the past decade, population has increased at an annual rate of from 3 to 3.5 percent, one of the highest in the world. In a poor country with limited ways of making a living, such overpopulation creates serious social as well as political problems. Some of these problems are described below.

Most of the people live in rural villages called *barrios* or *barangays*. (Only about 20 percent live in the cities.) The barrio or barangay is similar to an American township. Several barrios make up a *municipio* (municipality), and the commercial and administrative center—similar to a county seat—of a municipio is called a *pablacion.*

Earning a Living

Most Filipinos are farmers and live in rude huts made of bamboo and thatch. Since these can be easily destroyed by typhoons, many farm families try to earn and save enough money to be able to build a home made of cement blocks. An all-wooden home with a corrugated tin roof is something only the most well-to-do villagers can hope to attain. Electricity for illumination is rare. A single, un-

The Philippines contain many shantytowns similar to this one. Poverty is a major problem in the Philippines.

Even today, the majority of Philippine dwellings are built of bamboo and thatch.

shaded light bulb dangling from a cord in each room is a luxury.

The average farm family income is less than $500 a year, which is considered well below the national poverty level, which is about $1,200 a year. Rice and corn are the two most important crops. Sweet potatoes, yams, peanuts, cassava, and taro are grown for use in case the rice and corn crops fail. Family garden plots may also include string beans, tomatoes, onions, and other vegetables.

Until recent years, rice, which is the main food for three-quarters of the population, had to be imported. Today, the Philippines is a rice-exporting nation. This was brought about through the use of new, high-yield rice strains, irrigation projects, fertilizers, and pesticides. These technological advances took place under the Marcos administration, which borrowed billions of dollars, mainly from the United States, to improve the life of the Filipino farmer.

Through the U.S. Agency for International Development (AID), money has also been made available for new irrigation projects, to help make the land more productive. Since the 1970s, annual rice harvests have increased from an average of 1.5 to 3.3 tons for each hectare (2.4 acres). This means that many families can sell much of their rice for cash instead of using their harvest simply to feed themselves.

Nevertheless, poverty still persists. In fact, it seems to be growing even worse. In 1971, shortly before Marcos declared martial law, 44 percent of all Filipinos lived at or below the national poverty level. Today, 64 percent are below that level.

Why Poverty Persists

One of the main reasons for the continuing poverty is that there is simply not enough land for each farm family. In an attempt to remedy this situation, Marcos used some of the money he borrowed from other countries to buy millions of acres of land from landlords with large holdings. This land was then turned over to former tenant farmers, who were given low-interest government loans. But the exploding population growth still causes land to be scarce.

A farmer, for example, whose father owned seven hectares (17 acres) of land would divide that land among his seven children. This would give each child a single hectare on which to grow rice and corn. But each of those seven children might in turn have seven or more children, leaving virtually no land to be passed on to the next generation. This is typical of the land-owning situation in rural areas today, and is something which President Aquino hopes to change.

Corruption and inflation also drained off much of the money Marcos borrowed. Officials from the national level on down to the barrio level were all guilty of appropriating some of the foreign funds for themselves. This added to the unrest and resentment of the Marcos government. The meteoric rise in the price of oil also caused the cost of fertilizers to increase enormously, since many fertilizers are actually petroleum products. With the sudden drop in world oil prices early in 1986 there was some hope that this situation would be remedied, at least temporarily. But oil experts expected the price of petroleum to begin to rise again within the foreseeable future.

Even the cost of simple necessities has risen dramatically. Many farm families use kerosene for lamps to light their homes. A decade ago, a litre of kerosene cost one centavo (a tenth of a cent). Today, a litre of this fuel costs one peso and 70 centavos (17 cents).

The high cost of fuel has also sharply reduced the use of farm machinery. Few families or even groups of families could ever afford the initial investment needed to buy a tractor, but formerly one could be rented for a few pesos a day. Today, it costs the equivalent of $2 a day to rent such equipment—a prohibitive price for the average Filipino farmer. Consequently, the water buffalo remains the main beast of burden.

As a result of continued poverty and poor sanitation, many Filipinos suffer from malnutrition and disease. Tuberculosis, a major killer in rural areas, could probably be stamped out if medicines and nutritious foods were more widely and readily available.

The water buffalo remains the main beast of burden in the Philippines.

What the People Eat

Farm families raise almost all their own food. Few people buy much at the store other than salt. In addition to garden vegetables, a family may also raise chickens, but these, too, are considered something of a luxury and are frequently sold at the market. Nevertheless, chickens are a major source of protein. Dogs, which are considered a great delicacy, are also eaten on special occasions.

But meat, fish, and poultry are generally served only a few times a week and then only in small portions. All three daily meals are much the same and consist of rice, vegetables, and perhaps a piece of fruit—papaya, banana, or coconut. Occasionally, there are butter and eggs. Usually, there is a bunlike bread called *pan de sal.*

Education and Recreation

Education in the Philippines is compulsory through the sixth grade. But only about half of the Filipino children who enter first grade finish the sixth. This is because funds provided by the government are insufficient to supply free textbooks and other study materials as well as free lunches. Many elementary school children also drop out of school to help out on the family farm. School is where many Filipinos learn to speak English, because from the third grade on, English is the language of instruction.

Four-year secondary schools are largely privately financed, although there is some government funding. There are more than forty colleges and universities in the Philippines. But most of these are private, although the University of the Philippines is public. Several teachers colleges turn out more than enough teachers for the inadequate public school system. About a quarter of all secondary school graduates go on to college.

Recreation is extremely limited, consisting mainly of dances and local fiestas. Movies are found only in the cities. Spectator sports include baseball, soccer, basketball, boxing, and cockfighting, which is second only to jai alai in popularity. Jai alai is somewhat like handball, with the players using a basketlike scoop to catch and hurl the ball back against the court wall.

The game of jai alai. Jai alai uses a basket-like scoop to catch and hurl the ball back.

Home entertainment consists mainly of listening to the radio. Small transistor radios are highly prized; almost no farm families have television sets. Occasionally, some enterprising storekeeper in the village will buy a TV set to increase business in his or her establishment. Newspapers are popular and sell for only a few centavos. In the pre-Marcos period, freedom of the press was practiced. Under Marcos, the media were rigidly controlled and censored by the government.

Filipino Youth

With the general poverty and lack of opportunity in the villages, more and more young people in recent years have been leaving their homes. Their usual destination is the city, such as Manila, but many also go abroad.

The life they find in the cities, however, is hardly an improvement. In Manila, they often live in the slums along with a third of the rest of the city's population. Houses there are shanties made of flattened tin cans, cardboard, and scrap lumber. Life in the slums is also dangerous. To get out of this environment, it is necessary to obtain a high-paying job, but such jobs are few and far between.

A surprising number of people with college degrees live in the shantytowns. This is because jobs for professionals such as teachers, engineers, and scientists are hard to find and low paying. Literally thousands of degree-holding young people work in Manila for the equivalent of $100 a month or even less as store clerks, maids, or servants.

Many of these frustrated youths eventually decide to leave the Philippines entirely and take their chances abroad. This was encouraged by the Marcos government. Every young person who leaves the Philippines reduces the pressure on the domestic job market. In addition, the country obtains valuable foreign currency through the money that is sent home from young people overseas to their families. In 1983, some three-quarters of a million Filipinos working abroad sent $1 billion home to their families.

UNREST AT HOME

Obviously, such conditions of general poverty blight the daily lives of the people, both young and old, who continue to live in the Philippines. And this gloomy atmosphere breeds widespread political turmoil. Because the Marcos government was unable to improve the situation, the average Filipino began to turn to local revolutionary groups for more dramatic remedial action.

One of these groups is a kind of grass-roots guerrilla organization called the New People's Army, or NPA. The NPA is inclined to go its own way, ignoring local police and national army efforts to stamp out oppression and corruption. NPA leaders, in fact, regard the police and the military as part of the Philippines' problem of oppression, since it was their guns that kept the dictatorial Marcos government in power. On several occasions, small military detachments in remote rural areas have been ambushed and slain by NPA guerrillas. Although President Aquino hoped to reach some sort of cease-fire agreement and accommodation with the NPA, there were several slayings by them even after her inauguration.

The problem with the NPA, as the United States sees it, is that it is a communist organization, and the United States has long fought the spread of communism throughout the Pacific and in Southeast Asia. Marcos, too, was a long-time foe of communism. But by declaring martial law, which he said was necessary to stamp out the communists, he soon turned the Philippines into as oppressive a political government as that in any communist country.

After coming to power, Marcos tripled the size of the national army, but the red guerrillas have also grown in strength and boldness. They have even become aggressive enough to attack government troops, killing a number of them late in 1982 and early in 1983. During his election campaign in 1985 and 1986, Marcos claimed to have the NPA under control, but this was doubtful. What wasn't doubtful was the fact that President Aquino would also have to deal with the NPA as a major political problem.

WHO ARE THE NPA?

The NPA was originally a movement of college and university intellectuals. Today, it includes college students, workers, and a number of Catholic priests. The body of its guerrilla army, however, is made up of rural young men who are sick and tired of poverty, government corruption and oppression, and a continued lack of opportunity.

To date, the NPA has soft-pedaled its communist ties. This may be because of the Catholic priests in the organization. The Roman Catholic Church is a stout foe of communism, and since the Philippines is predominantly Catholic, the NPA does not want to emphasize this side of its background too strongly. The announced NPA political line is that it wants to better the life of the poor Filipino people. Of course, this is the traditional party line before communists assume control of a country.

But there is no flat denial on the part of the NPA leaders that theirs is a communist organization. What would actually occur if the NPA eventually came to power is not known. If it is indeed communist, greater oppression than ever would doubtless settle on the Philippines, for there are no greater oppressors in the world than true Soviet-style communists.

This, of course, is what the United States as well as the bulk of the Philippine people want to avoid. It is the main reason why the United States continued to support the anticommunist Marcos government for so long despite its obvious failings and broken promises.

President Aquino has never shown any fondness for Soviet-style communism either, but she has been sympathetic toward the NPA. Early in her presidential campaign she indicated she might place some NPA members in her cabinet if she were elected. After she was elected she ordered released all of those who had been put in jail as political prisoners by Marcos, including several top communist leaders. She also promised amnesty to all NPA members, claiming that, like herself, they were freedom fighters.

Whether or not President Aquino's attempts at reconciliation with these radical leftists will work is a serious question. Communist rebels in the Philippines want nothing less than total land reform, that is, the breaking up of the large sugar and coconut plantations and giving this land to the peasants. But it is doubtful if this drastic kind of reform can be accomplished without bloodshed. So the legacy of dictator Ferdinand Marcos was still very much a part of the new Philippines under reform-minded President Corazon Aquino.

3

THE RISE OF FERDINAND MARCOS

How does a heroic young freedom fighter turn into an aging military despot? That is a question many people asked about Ferdinand Marcos, sixth president of the Philippines since that country gained its independence from the United States in 1946.

Ferdinand Edralin Marcos was born in Sarrat in northern Luzon on September 11, 1917. His father was Mariano R. Marcos, a well-known lawyer and politician. His mother, Josea Edralin Marcos, was a schoolteacher. He was the oldest of four children.

Young Ferdinand's father was a strict disciplinarian who schooled the boy in athletics and the use of weapons. When Ferdinand was just sixteen, he won the small-bore rifle shooting championship of the Philippines. The elder Marcos also taught his son to be an accomplished speaker in three languages—English, Spanish, and Tagalog.

Until he was eight, young Ferdinand was educated by his mother both at home and in the one-room schoolhouse in Sarrat where she taught. In 1925, the elder Marcos was elected to the Philippine Congress, and the family moved to Manila. Young Marcos completed elementary

school and high school there, leading his class scholastically and excelling in sports.

From an early age Ferdinand had a remarkable memory. This stood him in good stead at the University of the Philippines, where books were scarce and available to each student for only short periods of time. His ability to quickly memorize pages in a book won him a scholarship to study law. He passed his bar examination in 1939 with a score of 98.01. This mark was so high that he was suspected of cheating. In response to these charges, young Marcos insisted that he be reexamined orally, and he passed this test with a score of 92.35.

At this point Ferdinand's meteoric career was brought to an abrupt though temporary halt when he was belatedly accused of having shot and killed Julio Nalundasan, a political rival of his father's, back in 1935. Nalundasan had been killed by a .22 caliber bullet. Young Marcos was known, of course, to be an expert with the .22, and he was also known to be fanatically loyal to his father. Why the charge against him came four years after the shooting was not clear, but it was suspected that there was a political motive behind it.

Nevertheless, in the fall of 1939, young Marcos was found guilty of being the trigger-man in the assassination. The case was immediately appealed to the Philippine Supreme Court, with Ferdinand himself arguing the appeal. In 1940, the verdict of guilty was reversed, and young Marcos joined his father's Manila law firm.

The trial and the youthful Marcos' successful self-defense brought him national attention. Many Filipinos regarded Ferdinand as a young hero whom political enemies of his father had tried to destroy. Soon Marcos was to become an even greater hero.

Marcos (far right) as a ten-year-old child with his family

THE PHILIPPINES' MOST DECORATED SOLDIER

The Japanese invaded the Philippines shortly after they attacked Pearl Harbor on December 7, 1941. Since the U.S. Pacific fleet had been all but destroyed in the Pearl Harbor attack, no immediate military assistance could be given to the Philippines. A relative handful of U.S. Regular Army soldiers and their Filipino allies fought on alone against the overwhelming superiority of the Japanese invasion forces. One of the most heroic of the Philippine defenders was Ferdinand Marcos, who was soon to become his country's most decorated soldier.

When the war began in the Pacific, Marcos was an intelligence officer working with the U.S. armed forces to gain secret information about the enemy. Soon the Americans and their Filipino allies were driven onto the narrow Bataan peninsula, where they set up a last-ditch defense. In the Bataan battle, Marcos was wounded and became one of the hundreds of prisoners captured by the Japanese when Bataan fell. The Japanese then forced these prisoners to go on a 200-mile (320-km) death march from Bataan to Camp O'Donnell in central Luzon. Almost a thousand thirst-crazed, starving Americans and Filipinos died on this march. Despite his wounds, Marcos survived.

Marcos also managed to survive the concentration camp conditions of Camp O'Donnell, where as many as three hundred prisoners died each day. When the Japanese discovered that Marcos had been an intelligence officer, they tortured him for more than a week, but he never gave them any secret information.

When he recovered from this ordeal, Marcos managed to escape and join the Filipino resistance forces. He soon became a guerrilla leader and established an organization known as the "Free Men." The Free Men gathered intelligence information and forwarded it to U.S. General Douglas MacArthur, who had managed to escape from the Philippines and establish headquarters in Australia. MacArthur had vowed to return and was already busy planning his strategy for liberating the Philippines. For his efforts in supplying the American forces with information they needed for their planned return, Marcos was awarded a Silver Star.

He won a second Silver Star when MacArthur and the U.S. forces did indeed return to the Philippines in 1944. By the end of the war, Marcos had been decorated with more than twenty Filipino and American medals, including the Distinguished Service Cross, and had attained the rank of colonel.

Doubts Cast on Marcos' Heroism

During Marcos' campaign against Corazon Aquino the *New York Times* published a report stating that according to U.S. Army records from the 1940s, Army investigators had found no proof of Marcos' claims that he had led a guerrilla group against the Japanese. The National Archives in Washington then made copies of these investigations public. In them it was stated that Marcos' claims that he had led such a guerrilla organization were "fraudulent" and "absurd."

Marcos' defenders, however, wondered why these documents had been buried in government archives for thirty-five years only to surface at this strategic moment. Others said they doubted that Marcos would have been awarded the Distinguished Service Cross, America's second highest award for valor, without a thorough investigation into his acts of heroism at the time.

POSTWAR ENTRY INTO POLITICS

After the war, Marcos resumed his law practice and soon came to be regarded as the Philippines' most successful trial lawyer. In 1947, as a member of the Philippines Veterans Commission, he succeeded in having Filipino war veterans accepted under the American G.I. Bill of Rights. This enabled them to get low-interest loans, receive money to go to college, and become eligible for numerous other benefits.

In 1949, Marcos decided to enter politics and thus follow in the footsteps of his father, who had been killed fighting the Japanese. Marcos first ran for the Philippine House of Representatives and won the election by a wide margin. He was reelected in 1953 and 1957.

As a congressman, Marcos introduced legislation reducing taxes on small landowners. He also became House minority leader and was the chairman of several key House committees. His record was so good that for ten straight years the Philippine Congressional Press Club named him as one of the outstanding congressmen.

In 1959, Marcos ran for the Senate. He won his election by the largest margin in the Republic's history. As a senator, Marcos was a champion of civil liberties, land reform, and the trade union movement. He was also a member of the Philippine delegation to the United Nations several times.

Marcos now had his eye on the presidency. But party leaders insisted that several older members deserved to get the nomination ahead of him. As a result, he left the Liberal party and joined the opposition—the Nationalist party. In 1964, the Nationalists nominated Marcos for president, and on November 9, 1965, he defeated his opponent, Diosdado Macapagal, by more than 650,000 votes. Actually, there was very little difference in the political goals of the two parties, as mentioned earlier. Voter preferences were made more on the basis of personalities than issues.

A PRESIDENT FOR REFORM

During his first term in office, Marcos was truly a president in favor of reform. He reduced waste in government spending by eliminating thousands of patronage jobs. Patronage jobs are jobs controlled by the party in power and awarded to loyal party members. He introduced land reform measures and authorized government subsidies to farmers. These measures took land away from large landowners and sold it to poor farmers at low prices. He fought crime and corruption both inside and outside government.

Marcos during his inauguration ceremonies as the new president of the Philippines in January 1966. Outgoing president Diosdado Macapagal is standing on the other platform. Marcos is dressed in a white, embroidered barong tagalag, a type of formal Philippine outerwear.

Then-Governor Ronald Reagan and his wife Nancy dance with Imelda and Ferdinand Marcos at a dinner given in the Reagans' honor on a visit to Manila in 1969. The Reagans became good friends of the Marcos'.

His efforts as a fighter against corruption, however, were hampered by the fact that graft had become so ingrained in Philippine politics that it was regarded by many as an acceptable way of life. For generations people had been paying bribes to politicians to obtain jobs, get taxes reduced, keep utilities working, and even to get favorable decisions in civil and criminal court cases.

One opposition group that arose to fight corruption in government was the communist Hukbalahaps, commonly called the Huks. The Huks favored the overthrow of the Philippine democratic government and wanted to replace it with a Marxist-Leninist communist regime. Marcos was fanatically opposed to the Huks—just as he later opposed the New People's Army—and in this he was staunchly backed by several U.S. presidential administrations.

Soon the United States was providing huge loans to help improve economic conditions in the Philippines and supporting Marcos in his efforts to stamp out the communists. He did this by declaring communist activity illegal and throwing active communists in jail. These efforts gradually all but abolished the Philippines' democratic government, and Marcos took over as a military dictator. But he did not do so without opposition. One of those who stoutly opposed him was Benigno Aquino.

BENIGNO AQUINO COMES ON THE SCENE

Benigno "Ninoy" Aquino had not fought in World War II. He was too young. But he did become a political hero to his people. Born in 1932 in Concepcion, north of Manila, Aquino was a member of a prominent family of politicians and plantation owners. Like Marcos, he became a lawyer-politician.

A political prodigy, Aquino had been elected mayor of his hometown of Concepcion when he was just twenty-two, and governor of his province, Tarlac, at the age of twenty-eight. When he was thirty-four, he was elected to the Philippine Senate and almost immediately became a political rival of Marcos. Aquino believed that Marcos was a dictator who had to be overthrown if human rights and civil liberties were to be restored.

Although Marcos had been elected president by a wide margin in 1965, Aquino's Liberal party staged a comeback and made a strong showing in the senatorial elections of 1971. According to public opinion polls, Aquino and his Liberals were strongly favored to regain control of the government in the next election, scheduled for 1973. Aquino himself would be running as the Liberal party's presidential candidate.

By a curious quirk of political fortune, however, Aquino would not be running against Marcos himself but rather Marcos' wife, Imelda. Since the Philippines was still operating under its old constitution, Marcos was not eligible to run for a third term, so it was expected that he would have his wife stand in for him.

It was at this point, in 1972, that Marcos confounded everybody by declaring martial law and having Aquino jailed. Aquino was charged with murder, subversive activity, and illegal possession of firearms. No evidence was presented to support these charges, however. Aquino was kept in jail at Fort Bonifacio near Manila until 1977, when he was finally convicted of all charges against him and sentenced to death. But his execution was delayed because of American objections to the Marcos regime's continued violations of human and civil rights. In 1980, Aquino was released on the condition that he go to the U.S. for corrective heart surgery.

In the United States, Aquino successfully underwent a heart bypass operation in Dallas. When he recovered, he obtained research fellowships at Harvard and the Massachusetts Institute of Technology. But his mended heart was still in the Philippines. He could not return there, however, for fear of once again being thrown into jail. In the end, his patriotism and his growing opposition to the Marcos government made him decide to risk returning to his homeland.

In 1983, when Aquino decided to return to the Philippines, President Marcos sent his wife, Imelda, to New

Detained Senator Benigno Aquino argues his case before the Supreme Court. He was eventually sentenced to die by firing squad, but his sentence was commuted because of pressure from the United States.

York to try to persuade Aquino to change his mind. By now, the exiled Aquino had become a popular hero to the Filipinos, and Marcos feared that his return would result in antigovernment demonstrations. In a lengthy meeting at the Philippines consulate in New York, Imelda relayed her husband's warning about the threat to Aquino's life and told him, "Think of your family for a change. You can all remain in New York and enjoy life." Aquino told friends that through Imelda Marcos he had been offered any amount of money he wanted to support himself, his wife Corazon, and their family of five children as long as he stayed in the United States.

Not only did Aquino refuse the offer, but he calmly accepted the threat to his life and returned to the Philippines prepared, if necessary, to die. Comparing himself to another, earlier Filipino martyr, José B. Rizal, who returned from exile in 1892 only to eventually be executed by the Spanish, Aquino told reporters who accompanied him on the plane to his homeland, "If I should die at the hand of the oppressors, let it be."

IMELDA MARCOS, THE "IRON BUTTERFLY"

Imelda Marcos is one of the most interesting and powerful women in Philippine history. As ambitious and ruthless a politician as her husband, Imelda Marcos was known to many Filipinos as the "Iron Butterfly."

Ferdinand Marcos and Imelda Romualdez of Tacloban, Leyte, were married in 1954. The Romualdez family was one of the wealthiest and most influential families in the Philippines. Among her relatives were judges, governors, and provincial administrators who controlled more than half a million votes in the central part of the Republic.

Imelda's immediate family, however, was quite poor, and Imelda resented the fact that they had to depend on support from their rich relations. At an early age she determined she would one day be rich herself. This childhood frustration over lack of money may have caused her excessive greed as First Lady of the Philippines.

Imelda had little formal education, but she had strong political interests. She was also a great beauty, and as the "Rose of Tacloban" (after her hometown) was named Miss Manila the same year she and the dashing young congressman, Ferdinand Marcos, were married. She is thirteen years younger than her husband.

From the very beginning of their marriage, Imelda Marcos proved to be a big help to her husband's political career. During his campaigns for the senate and the presidency, she accompanied him, making emotional speeches and singing songs to entertain the voters. Aquino once observed that the Iron Butterfly was worth a million votes to her husband.

There are three Marcos children—a son, Ferdinand, Jr., and two daughters, Maria Imelda; and Maria Victoria.

At first, Imelda Marcos claimed she had no political ambitions of her own, but soon after her husband declared martial law this attitude began to change. Marcos named her governor of metropolitan Manila and appointed her to the fifteen-member executive committee. This powerful panel advised Marcos on all government decisions and had the right to decide who would succeed him if he died in office or simply resigned. But with her husband's defeat by Corazon Aquino and the Marcos' sudden flight into exile, Imelda's power in Philippine politics became a thing of the past and a matter of purely historical interest.

In order to fully understand the modern history of the Philippines, it is important to know something about the early days of the Philippines' long fight for freedom and democracy. The members of the Marcos regime were not the first oppressors with whom the freedom-loving Filipinos had to do battle.

4

EARLY HISTORY OF THE PHILIPPINES

Probably the first people to occupy the Philippines were the Negritos, some 25,000 years ago. It is not known for sure where they came from. The Negritos were followed by Indonesians and Malays from the East Indies. This was several hundred years before the birth of Christ. During the next several centuries, trade developed between the Philippines and China, and many Chinese also later settled on the islands. Still later, Moslem Arab missionaries arrived and converted the Moros of Mindanao Island to Islam, the Moslem religion. The whole of the Philippines might today be an Arab or Oriental nation had it not been for the arrival of the Spanish in the sixteenth century.

In 1521, explorer Ferdinand Magellan on his round-the-world voyage anchored the Spanish fleet in Cebu harbor. Magellan and his men became friendly with the people of Cebu Island and aided them in an invasion of neighboring Mactan Island. Magellan was killed in this action, but the rest of his crew later went on to complete the historic first voyage around the world. Also, at a later time, the Philippines were named after King Philip II of Spain.

Magellan's first contact with the Philippines was soon followed by several Spanish colonizing expeditions. The

Spanish were seeking rare spices and attempting to expand their empire into Southeast Asia. These colonizing expeditions brought with them many Spanish priests and friars, who set about converting the Filipinos, whom they called "Indios," to Roman Catholicism. Few rare spices were found in the Philippines, but the islands were a fertile field for religious conversions. Even many of the Chinese merchants there were converted to Roman Catholicism.

Many of these converted Chinese married Filipino women, and there were numerous other racially mixed marriages. Their descendants were known as *mestizos*, or people of mixed blood. When the Spanish took control of the islands, the mestizos became a wealthy merchant and plantation-owning class who sent their children abroad to school. These well-educated youths came to be called *ilustrados*, or enlightened ones, and when they returned to their homeland they began to demand social change and more of a say in the government of the Philippines. These were the first signs of nationalism and a desire for independence among the Filipinos.

JOSÉ RIZAL, FIRST FILIPINO MARTYR

While studying in Europe in the late nineteenth century, a group of young ilustrados formed a Philippine independence organization. The first leader of this group, which was called simply the "Propaganda Movement," was a young intellectual named José B. Rizal. Rizal came to believe that a revolution was needed to gain independence for the Philippines.

Rizal and the other members of the Propaganda Movement were beaten to the punch, however, by a young revolutionary back in the Philippines named Andrés Bonifacio. Bonifacio was not an ilustrado. In fact, he had very little education. He worked as a clerk in a store in Manila. But within him the fires of freedom burned brightly.

Bonifacio organized a secret revolutionary society named *Katipunan*, or "Sons of the People." Unsupported by the ilustrados, Bonifacio led his young revolutionaries in a rebellion against the Spanish authorities in San Juan del Monte province in the summer of 1896. Meanwhile, Rizal had returned to the Philippines, where news of his own revolutionary intentions preceded his arrival. Though neither Rizal nor any other ilustrado backed the Katipunan movement, Rizal was seized and thrown in jail when the Katipunan rebellion broke out.

Rizal was held in jail until the end of the year. Then, on December 30, 1896, he was executed by a firing squad.

Rizal's execution caused the Katipunan and ilustrado forces to unite. But a power struggle then began between Bonifacio and a rising young military leader named Emilio Aguinaldo. Bonifacio was killed in the struggle and Aguinaldo emerged as the undisputed leader of the Filipino revolutionary forces.

The revolutionary forces, however, had been badly weakened in their fight with one another. The Spanish took advantage of this situation by offering to grant amnesty to the revolutionaries and pay Aguinaldo and some of his followers a large sum of money if he would voluntarily go into exile. They also promised certain political reforms that were never actually put into practice. Aguinaldo accepted this offer late in 1897, and he and his aides left for Hong Kong, where they awaited a favorable opportunity to return to the Philippines.

THE SPANISH-AMERICAN WAR: ENTER THE UNITED STATES

In the spring of 1898, the United States and Spain went to war. The dispute was over Cuba. Years of Spanish misrule of that island had caused the Cubans to rebel against Spain in 1895. The United States sympathized with the rebels, and there was much talk—especially in the American press—about the United States intervening in the revolution.

Earlier, the United States had tried to buy Cuba from Spain. When this offer was refused, American efforts to set Cuba free continued. The Cuban revolution seemed like an ideal chance to force the Spanish to grant Cuba

Emilio Aguinaldo (on horseback) in 1916

its independence. While considering armed intervention in the conflict, the United States sent the battleship *Maine* into Cuba's Havana harbor.

On the night of February 15, 1898, the *Maine* blew up, killing 260 American sailors. To this day, it is not known who or what caused the explosion, but the American press accused Spain of the act. "Remember the Maine!" soon became a nationwide battlecry, and on April 25, 1898, war was declared by the United States against Spain.

WAR BEGINS IN THE PHILIPPINES

The first battle of the Spanish-American War did not take place in Cuba, however, but in the far-off Philippines. Certain that with the sinking of the *Maine* war with Spain was imminent, Assistant Secretary of the Navy Theodore Roosevelt had placed Commodore George Dewey in command of the U.S. Asiatic fleet and told him to prepare the fleet for action in the Philippines. According to legend, when told of Roosevelt's orders, President William McKinley commented that he knew that Spain owned the Philippines but confessed he wasn't sure where they were.

A week after the United States declared war on Spain, McKinley knew where the Philippines were. In fact, the whole world knew, for they were the scene of one of the most decisive, one-sided naval battles in the history of sea warfare.

Early on the Sunday morning of May 1, 1898, Commodore Dewey's U.S. Asiatic fleet steamed into Manila Bay, where a large part of the Spanish Pacific war fleet was stationed. When the Spanish ships came within range, Dewey told the captain of the flagship *Olympia*, "You may fire when ready, Gridley."

A few hours later, ten of Spain's major warships were sunk and several hundred Spanish sailors were dead. No American ships were badly damaged, and no American lives were lost.

With this action, the United States began to play an important role in the history of the Philippines.

Above: *the* U.S.S. Maine *sinking after a series of explosions on February 15, 1898, in Havana Harbor*
Opposite: *Commodore George Dewey*

THE RETURN OF EMILIO AGUINALDO

When he learned of the defeat of the Spanish war fleet in Manila Bay, the exiled revolutionary Emilio Aguinaldo immediately returned to the Philippines to lead a revolution against Spain. The Filipinos heralded Aguinaldo's return and rallied to his side. Independence seemed to be at hand. Aguinaldo, of course, having received arms from the U.S. government, expected full support from the United States in his and his people's declaration of independence. In this he was to be severely disappointed.

Soon after President McKinley learned the location of the Philippine Islands, he began to realize their strategic importance. Control of them would make the United States both a major power in the Pacific and a world power. Although there was some loud public opposition to the United States becoming an imperialist nation, McKinley and other government officials began to make plans to take over, or annex, the Philippines. When he got wind of these plans, Aguinaldo prepared to fight the United States.

The Spanish-American War was a short conflict and ended in complete victory for the United States. The Philippines thus became the first and only colony the United States ever had. In Cuba, the first American troops landed on the coast in June of 1898, and the last fighting occurred with the Spanish surrender of Santiago on July 17. Spain agreed to an armistice on August 12. Formal fighting in the Philippines ended a few days later, and a peace treaty was signed in Paris on December 10, 1898. Spain granted Cuba its independence and ceded the Philippines to the United States. In return for the Philippines, the U.S. paid Spain $20 million.

THE PHILIPPINE INSURRECTION

Aguinaldo and his Filipino followers refused to accept U.S. control of the Philippines. They bitterly resented their country's having been "bought" for a few million dollars,

A U.S. marine detachment, in May 1898, runs up the first American flag ever to be raised in the Philippines.

and they were determined to continue their fight for freedom. On January 23, 1899, in the town of Malolos, a national constitution was proclaimed, and Aguinaldo was elected president of the new Republic of the Philippines.

The United States government regarded this establishment of a separate government as unlawful. President McKinley called it an insurrection—somewhat as if an American state had defied the federal government—and labeled Aguinaldo and his followers insurrectionists, or *insurrectos.* The president ordered General Elwell S. Otis and his U.S. Army troops who were still in Manila following the Spanish surrender to capture or kill Aguinaldo and put down the insurrection.

At Malolos, which was about 30 miles (48 km) from Manila, Aguinaldo had between 30,000 and 50,000 insurrecto troops. The American forces in Manila numbered only about 12,000 or 14,000. But the insurrectos were poorly armed and lacked ammunition for the few guns they had. Many Filipinos were armed only with spears or machete-like bolo knives.

Aguinaldo and his insurrectos had one major advantage. Many of them were stationed in blockhouses surrounding Manila. The major U.S. advantage was its naval warships stationed in Manila harbor, against which the Filipinos had no defense. Most of the fighting during the insurrection took place on the island of Luzon.

THE FIGHTING BEGINS

Fighting began on February 4, 1899, when the insurrectos attacked Manila. The Americans fought back fiercely and on the following day launched a counterattack. One of the two U.S. divisions that took part in this counterattack was led by General Arthur MacArthur, father of World War II hero Douglas MacArthur.

The American forces were supported by artillery, Gatling guns—forerunner of the machine gun—and ships' guns from the U.S. Navy. The fighting lasted for two days, and when it was over the insurrecto forces were shattered and in full retreat. They had suffered more than 3,000 casualties, the United States about 250. General Otis prepared to inform Washington that the insurrection had been put down and that the fight for the Philippines had ended. Otis did not send the message, however, because he and his men soon realized that the fight had just started.

The insurrectos now engaged the American troops in guerrilla-style warfare. The roadless, tropical, heavily forested Philippines—like Vietnam some sixty years later—was ideal for guerrilla fighting. It was impossible for the Americans to mount a major offensive against small bands of Filipinos who struck secretly, often by night, or set up ambushes during the day along jungle trails, attacked silently, and then faded into the tropical forests. Artillery and naval guns were useless against such furtive attackers. The heavy Gatling guns could not be hauled through the thick forest undergrowth.

General Otis had been trained in traditional warfare, and he continued to try orthodox methods of fighting the guerrillas. During the next seven months, an additional 35,000 U.S. troops arrived in the Philippines and Otis continued to waste them in futile attacks on an enemy that refused to fight in open battle. The Filipinos—again as the Vietcong guerrillas would later do in Vietnam—stealthily cut the Americans down by eating away at their flanks, killing a handful of men here, another handful there, with silent, murderous swings of their bolo knives, or by dropping them a man at a time with spears hurled from out of nowhere. As casualties mounted morale among the Americans began to deteriorate, and the fighting seemed to go on both endlessly and futilely.

Nevertheless, with its enormously superior manpower and firepower, General MacArthur's division was able to capture Aguinaldo's headquarters at Malolos. But Aguinaldo had already fled and was rallying his scattered forces elsewhere in the jungle. A victory without the capture of Aguinaldo was an empty one, so the guerrilla warfare continued. To make matters worse, soon the rainy season had set in, and it was impossible for the United States to even attempt to resume any full-scale fighting until the autumn of 1899.

PRESIDENT MCKINLEY TAKES A HAND

Among the U.S. military forces in the Philippines were a few officers and enlisted men to whom guerrilla warfare was somewhat familiar. These were the soldiers who had fought the American Indians in the West and Southwest. They had learned that success in guerrilla warfare depended on speed, daring, cunning, surprise, and, perhaps most important, attacking the enemy with small, highly mobile bodies of men.

One of these officers who had become highly skilled in frontier fighting against the Indians was a small, wiry, red-haired colonel named Frederick Funston. Funston now determined to use his own guerrilla skills and those of a handful of his Twentieth Regiment of Kansas volunteers to capture Aguinaldo. But Funston could not get permission from General Otis to lead a small raiding party into insurrecto territory.

General Otis was still determined to defeat the insurrectos in open battle, and when the dry season began in October of 1899, he resumed his full-scale assault. During the next year, several hundred separate engagements were fought, but at the end of this time the insurrectos seemed to be as strong and as invincible as ever.

At this point President McKinley decided to take a hand in solving the problem. He appointed a civil governor to try to bring order out of the chaos of the Philippines. The man he appointed was William Howard Taft, a future U.S. president.

Taft was as able a man as he was big—he weighed some 300 pounds (135 kg)—and when he arrived in the Philippines in the spring of 1900 he immediately went to work. General Otis' resignation was accepted, and General MacArthur was named to replace him. While MacArthur formulated military plans to subdue the insurrectionists, Taft went about his business devising civil plans to subdue them. Schools were built, villages were restored, medical aid was made available, and a modest form of self-government was established among the civilian population. To receive these benefits, however, the Filipinos had to take an oath of allegiance to the United States. Most were happy to do so, although a large body of insurrectos still remained at large and fought any attempts to establish a civil government. Taft and MacArthur both knew that the American efforts could never be wholly successful as long as Aguinaldo remained at large.

THE CAPTURE OF AGUINALDO

Early in 1901, Funston—a general officer now—presented his raiding party plan to General MacArthur. MacArthur immediately approved it. A few days later, Funston's men captured an insurrecto messenger named Cecilio Segismundo and persuaded him to tell them where Aguinaldo's headquarters were now located. Segismundo, who was weary of the war, told them Aguinaldo was in a village named Palanan in northeastern Luzon. He also agreed to lead them there. Funston then devised an ingenious plan to capture Aguinaldo.

Segismundo, it turned out, was not the only insurrecto who was war-weary. Many insurrectos, Segismundo said, wanted to surrender to the Americans, but they were fearful of being killed if they did so. Funston told Segismundo to get together a party of these defecting insurrectos and bring them to U.S. headquarters. When this was done, Funston made up a story that he hoped Aguinaldo would believe. Funston told Segismundo to notify Aguinaldo that some insurrecto troops had captured five American officers and that Segismundo and the insurrectos were bringing them to Aguinaldo's headquarters. Aguinaldo's reply indicated that he would be delighted to receive such important prisoners. Funston and four of his hand-picked officers, pretending to be prisoners, then set out for Palanan accompanied by Segismundo and the band of insurrecto defectors acting as their "guards." The party left Manila on February 11, 1901.

The trip to Palanan was the most difficult part of the capture of Aguinaldo. It took Funston, his men, and their "guards" almost two months to complete the journey through some of the most rugged jungle country in the Philippines.

Once they arrived, however, there was only a brief struggle with Aguinaldo's guards before the mission was accomplished. During the struggle, Funston's men wanted to kill Aguinaldo, but Funston threw himself on top of the rebel leader to protect him and ordered his men to hold their fire. A few weeks later, Aguinaldo was returned to Manila.

The capture of Aguinaldo broke the back of the insurrection, although small bands of insurrectos carried on the fighting for many months. Ironically, Aguinaldo was only in captivity a short time before he gave his oath of allegiance to the United States.

The Philippine insurrection did not formally end until July 4, 1902. On that date a proclamation that hostilities had ceased was signed by a new U.S. president. Since the new president had been a key person in starting hostilities against the Philippines, it was perhaps fitting that he should officially end them. His name was Theodore Roosevelt.

5

MODERN HISTORY OF THE PHILIPPINES

Soon after the United States gained complete control of the Philippines, it began to make plans for their independence as a republic. Unfortunately, these plans took almost half a century to be implemented. This was because there were many American government officials who believed that the "little brown brother," as the Philippine people were condescendingly called, had to grow up and prepare themselves for independence.

In the interim, the United States governed the islands through a five-man commission headed by a civil governor, William Howard Taft. The commission gave many responsible island government jobs to the ilustrados. Many additional Filipinos also gained authority in the national legislature or assembly, which was established in 1907. In 1916, the commission was replaced by an elected House and Senate. Finally, in 1934, the U.S. Congress passed the Tydings-McDuffie Act, which said that the Philippines would be given complete independence after ten years of successful self-government.

The following year, 1935, the Commonwealth of the Philippines was established, and Manuel L. Quezon was elected its first president. During World War II, when the

Japanese took over the Philippines, Quezon formed a government in exile in Washington, D.C. He died in 1944 and was succeeded by Sergio Osmena. Quezon City, just northeast of Manila, was named in honor of Quezon and served temporarily as the nation's capital.

THE JAPANESE OCCUPATION OF THE PHILIPPINES

The Philippines suffered severely at the hands of the Japanese during World War II. When they first took over the islands in January of 1942, the Japanese made a show of being friendly toward the Filipinos. They played up the fact that they were all Oriental brothers and sisters who should be opposed to the white imperialistic Americans. Of course, having the Filipinos on their side would have helped the Japanese in fighting the war. A friendly Philippines would have eliminated the need for stationing large forces of occupation troops there.

To prove their good intentions, the Japanese freed many of the Filipino troops who had fought against them on Bataan and encouraged them to take up arms against the Americans. Few did so. They, as well as most other Filipinos, were skeptical of these gestures of friendship. But a small number of civilians readily accepted them and began to collaborate with the enemy. Many of these collaborators were well-to-do Filipinos who hoped to curry favor with the Japanese and thus gain additional food and other privileges. This situation would eventually cause a radical split in postwar Philippine society.

Meanwhile, the Japanese shrewdly took advantage of the Filipino nationalistic desire for independence by declaring the Philippines an independent republic in 1943. This move won additional converts. But the Filipino skeptics pointed out that the so-called "independent republic" was a sham. The new government had not been elected,

Manuel Quezon

and the new president, José P. Laurel, was a collaborator chosen for the job by the Japanese military authorities.

It was not long before the Japanese occupation forces showed their true colors. Press censorship was absolute, listening to foreign radio broadcasts was forbidden under penalty of death, failure to cooperate with the Japanese military government also became a capital crime, and valueless money was forced on the civilian populace. When the conquerors confiscated all available rice, a famine on Luzon resulted.

Japanese army troops were especially brutal in their treatment of Filipino civilians, but their crimes of rape and looting went unpunished by the occupation authorities. Soon, Filipino civilians began to take matters into their own hands, ambushing Japanese soldiers by night and killing them. Reprisals were swift and murderous, with some villages being entirely wiped out. Such actions only fanned the flames of Filipino desire to free themselves from their Japanese oppressors. Soon guerrilla bands were formed—among them the Free Men in which Marcos was active—and the Japanese found themselves engaged in costly guerrilla warfare.

Guerrillas Loyal to MacArthur

One of the main problems the guerrillas had was a lack of weapons. At first, less than a quarter of them were armed with guns. Ammunition had to be severely rationed, with only a few rounds going to each man. Food was scarce. But the guerrillas held one solid advantage over the enemy. That was in their thorough knowledge of the countryside. They could disappear into the jungle or mountains and remain hidden for weeks and months, appearing only occasionally to attack a small party of Japanese. Often these attacks were waged by night, the guerrillas wielding their ancient bolo knives with the same deadly efficiency that their fathers and grandfathers had displayed during the Spanish-American War. Only this time, they were fighting on the side of the Americans.

American friendship had come to mean a great deal to many Filipinos. The Americans had proved themselves to be loyal and fair administrators of the Philippines, even if they had not granted the island republic its independence as soon as many would have liked.

One radical nationalist, Tomas Confesor, went so far as to say, "We have been living during the last forty years under a regime of justice and liberty."

The physical embodiment and living symbol of America's just treatment was Douglas MacArthur, son of General Arthur MacArthur. After the Spanish-American War, Arthur MacArthur had helped to administer the Philippines, and he had bred into his son, Douglas, a love of the Filipinos and a respect for their institutions.

Douglas MacArthur, like his father, was a graduate of West Point. His first assignment after graduation in 1903 was in the Philippines. Eventually, he would serve four "hitches," or tours of duty, there and come to regard the Philippines as an American trust to be administered fairly and with justice and respect.

Early in his tour of duty in the Philippines, MacArthur became friends with Manuel Quezon, former guerrilla and future president, but that friendship was interrupted by the Japanese invasion. Quezon fled to the United States and MacArthur to Australia, but both men vowed to return. Only death would prevent Quezon from fulfilling his vow; nothing would stop MacArthur.

When he left the Philippines for Australia, MacArthur solemnly stated, "I shall return!" This declaration instantly became a famous wartime battlecry not only in the Philippines but also in the United States. Filipinos universally believed that the United States and MacArthur would live up to the general's word. Vincente Raval, a guerrilla leader and aide to Marcos, later said: "We had total faith in the American promise to come back. We never faltered in our hope."

Aid from MacArthur

When MacArthur left the Philippines, he was not aware of the resistance activity there. But after many weeks, Marcos and his Free Men managed to piece together a shortwave radio and began to broadcast an appeal for aid to MacArthur in Australia. Almost immediately MacArthur began to dispatch arms, ammunition, and other supplies by submarine to the Philippines. At first, these supplies were limited, but within a few months several of the U.S. Navy's largest submarines were making deliveries to the guerrillas of up to 50 tons per trip. Soon, the guerrilla cause began to look brighter.

As the guerrillas became better able to carry on their harassment of the enemy, their ranks swelled. By war's end, they would number some 250,000 and be supported by almost the entire civilian population of the Philippines.

A surprising number of the new guerrilla recruits were American. These men were members of the U.S. armed forces who had escaped from Bataan. They fled into the mountains and jungles and somehow managed to survive until they could make their first contact with friendly Filipino allies. Several of these Americans proved to be outstanding guerrilla leaders.

Vital Guerrilla Activities

If MacArthur and his forces were to successfully reinvade the Philippines, what the general needed was specific information on Japanese troop locations and troop and ship movements. To obtain this intelligence information, it was essential that the guerrillas establish observation posts and coast-watcher stations. Then, of course, the information had to be coded and transmitted by radio to Australia.

Getting radios to the guerrillas became a top priority, and when the radios began to arrive in the Philippines, the Americans among the guerrillas were put in charge of encoding the messages. Within a matter of months, a regular transmission network had been set up throughout the islands, and several thousand reports were being sent to MacArthur each month.

Ferdinand Marcos and his Free Men played a key role in gathering intelligence for transmission over this radio network. Marcos had begun working in the Manila underground resistance and had rapidly become famous for his courageous and daring exploits. To avoid detection by the Japanese, he had faked his own death soon after the enemy occupation and even had a false death certificate placed in the Manila city records. One of his aides went even further and had a tombstone with his name on it placed in a prominent place in a local cemetery. For much of the war, among members of his immediate family, only Marcos' mother knew that Ferdinand was alive.

Having been among the first of the guerrillas to establish radio contact with MacArthur, Marcos continued to work closely with the general's headquarters throughout the war. When MacArthur asked the guerrillas to cut back on their ambushing activities against the Japanese and concentrate instead on gathering military intelligence, it was Marcos who put the general's wishes into effect. Many guerrillas preferred killing Japanese to manning isolated coast-watcher stations and reporting on Japanese ship movements, but Marcos saw to it that they obeyed orders.

MacArthur was also concerned that as the strength of the guerrilla forces grew, they might decide to take matters into their own hands and engage the Japanese occupation troops in open battle. This, MacArthur knew, would be suicidal. What he wanted was for the guerrillas to lie low until the United States actually invaded the Philippines and to then stage an uprising. Marcos was instrumental in the accomplishment of this difficult task as well.

Actually, there was considerable danger involved in manning lonely observation posts or coast-watcher stations. As this activity grew, and radio traffic grew with it, the Japanese became fully aware of what was going on. They also became increasingly efficient in combatting it. Radio direction finders were used to pinpoint secret radios, with Japanese troops then being sent in to destroy the sending stations and their occupants. Many guerrillas and several important guerrilla leaders were killed in this fashion. But the intelligence effort never ceased. Operators moved about frequently, never transmitting from the same place twice, and whenever operators were apprehended and killed, new volunteers stepped forward to take their place.

MacArthur's Return to the Philippines

In the autumn of 1944, U.S. warplanes taking off from aircraft carriers lying just off the coast began a preinvasion "softening up" of the Philippines. These bombers paved the way for MacArthur's long-heralded return, and the Filipino guerrillas were delighted to see that their intelligence-gathering efforts were at long last paying off. Straight as arrows, the American bombers headed toward Japanese targets identified by the underground guerrillas. Camouflaged ammunition and supply dumps, airfields hidden away in the jungles, Japanese headquarters and communications buildings disguised as civilian dwelling places—all were blasted by the relentless attackers.

It was expected that MacArthur would first come ashore at Mindanao. Instead, he chose Leyte, where American forces began landing in strength on October 20, 1944. MacArthur remained aboard the cruiser *Nashville* while Sixth Army troops made an early morning amphibious landing. When the troops had advanced inland a few thousand feet, MacArthur and his aides boarded a landing craft and headed toward shore. Some 35 yards (32 m) offshore, the landing craft went aground, and MacArthur and his party had to get out and walk. The water was only up to their knees, and a photographer recorded the event in one of the war's most memorable pictures.

After the war, General MacArthur said: "It took me only thirty or forty long strides to reach dry land, but that was one of the most meaningful walks I ever took."

A short time later, MacArthur broadcast his return over the nation's radio network, calling on citizens and guerrillas alike to "rise and strike" the Japanese oppressors. This they did, and with their aid the U.S. infantry, supported by fighter and bomber aircraft, swept away all enemy forces before them. The war, of course, would not end for almost another full year, but the United States and

General Douglas MacArthur (left) returns to the Philippines, as promised, disembarks from his landing craft, and wades ashore on Leyte Island with his detachment of soldiers in October 1944.

General MacArthur had kept their faith with the Philippine people.

THE POSTWAR PHILIPPINES

The United States further lived up to its pledge to the Philippines when it granted that nation its independence on July 4, 1946. Manuel Roxas was elected the first president. Roxas had played an important and risky role during the war. He had remained in Manila posing as a collaborator but secretly passing vital information to Marcos, who relayed it to MacArthur in Australia and Quezon in Washington. When his activities became known after the war, Roxas became a national hero. Unfortunately, he died in 1948, and Elpidio Quirino succeeded him as president. Other Filipinos who had actually collaborated with the Japanese were now accused of disloyalty, but few were actually tried for treason. In fact, many former collaborators went on to gain important positions in the postwar government. This caused great resentment on the part of loyal Filipinos and resulted in a split in society that has not been healed to this day.

During the postwar period, the Philippines had a long and difficult struggle to rebuild from the ravages of war. Manila as well as several other cities had been largely destroyed, and there was a continuing food shortage. The new nation was greatly aided by the United States, which sent $1 billion in economic assistance between 1946 and 1951. Millions of additional dollars were sent over the next three decades.

The Huk Rebellion

The new government of the Philippines was severely hampered during this postwar rebuilding period by the so-called Huks, who tried to overthrow the U.S.-sponsored

Independence Day,
July 4, 1946,
in the Philippines

Ramon Magsaysay with a crowd of well-wishers

regime. The communist Huks had a 20,000-man army, which tried to seize the government, but after several years of fighting, the Philippine army managed to put down the rebellion—temporarily.

One of the leaders in the fight against the Huks was Ramon Magsaysay. Magsaysay was elected president to succeed Quirino in 1953. Magsaysay was a staunch believer in human rights for all Filipinos—not just the favored rich—and was instrumental in passing important land reform legislation in an attempt to break up the huge plantations to help poor farmers. Magsaysay was aided in this reform movement by Benigno Aquino.

Unfortunately, Magsaysay was killed in an airplane crash in the spring of 1957. He was succeeded by Carlos P. Garcia. Garcia was a political moderate, who tried to slow the reform movement and thus appease the protesting large landowners. General dissatisfaction with his efforts led to his being defeated by the Liberal party's candidate, Diosdado Macapagal, in 1961. It was Macapagal whom Marcos defeated in 1965 to begin his long, controversial reign as president of the Philippines—a reign that saw the mercurial Marcos mysteriously change from liberal reformer to political despot.

Resumption of the Huk Rebellion Leads to Martial Law

Marcos was scarcely sworn into office before the Huk rebellion was resumed. This time, the Huks were supported by students demanding educational reforms and farmers and workers demanding agriculture and labor reforms.

Since the students, farmers, and laborers were sympathetic to the Huks, Marcos labeled them all communists and insisted that a "Red Revolution" was trying to overthrow the lawful Philippine government and replace it with a Marxist-Leninist socialist regime. This gave Marcos an excuse to declare martial law, which resulted in virtually the complete loss of democratic freedoms, freedoms that the Philippine Republic is today trying to restore under its new president, Corazon Aquino.

6

THE FUTURE OF THE PHILIPPINES

Although Corazon Aquino accomplished a seemingly impossible task in becoming President of the Republic of the Philippines, the difficulties she faced in governing the country seemed, if anything, even more impossible. Her number one problem was reviving the Philippine economy. Long known as "the sick man of Asia," the Philippines under Marcos had suffered a drastic decline in foreign trade and was existing mainly on foreign loans. (Aquino herself had said during her campaign, "The Philippine economy is a 'basket case'.") Unless President Aquino could reverse this trend and bring about an economic revival, she probably would not be able to solve many of her nation's other problems.

And these problems are indeed many. They include skyrocketing monetary inflation, an urgent need for welfare reform, land reform, political reform, and rebuilding the military and reviving its morale, which fell to an all-time low during the final days of the Marcos regime. None of these problems can be solved quickly.

In the matter of foreign debt, which ranges anywhere from $22 billion to $30 billion, depending upon who is doing the estimating, the International Monetary Fund

(IMF) gave some indication that it might ease up on its stiff repayment terms as it had done earlier in South America. In fact, shortly after President Aquino assumed control of the government, IMF officials journeyed to the Philippines to reassess the financial situation there. In addition, the Reagan Administration and the U.S. Congress gave every indication that it would extend additional financial aid. "If we want this experiment to be a success," said Senator Richard Lugar, who had helped monitor the Philippine presidential elections, "we're going to have to do more."

The Philippines gained its "sick man of Asia" label because it is the only Asian country with a shrinking economy. The total value of its annual output of goods and services, or gross national product (GNP), declined some 10 percent during the last two years of the Marcos regime, while other Third World countries such as South Korea and Taiwan prospered.

When President Aquino took office, some 70 percent of the population of the Philippines lived in poverty. In the three years before Aquino took office there had been a 15 percent drop in per capita income. With 22 percent of the work force unemployed and 40 percent employed in jobs below their skill level, it is clear why both jobs and a new national welfare plan are essential. Even those who do work earn only a few hundred dollars a year; thus inflation, which had been running between 25 and 30 percent annually, is a critical problem.

To restructure the nation's economy Aquino named Jaime Ongpin as finance minister. Ongpin is highly regarded in Western business circles. He had also been one of Marcos' harshest critics and was expected to wage a quiet revolution in the Philippines' economic system.

THE COMMUNIST INSURGENCY AND LAND REFORM

Land reform is closely related to political reform, and to the problem of the NPA, or "communist insurgency," as it is generally called. Although she did not put any communists in her presidential cabinet, as she originally said she would, Aquino did keep her promise to pardon all political prisoners. Among these political prisoners were several top communist leaders, whom most of her advisers said she should keep in jail. They included Jose Maria Sison, founder of the outlawed Communist party; Bernabe Buscayno, founder of the New People's Army, the communists' guerrilla arm; and several members of a rebel assassination squad.

In addition, the new president declared a six-month amnesty for all communists and NPA members during which all previous crimes against the government, including murder, would be forgiven. The Aquino government also said it would buy all NPA weapons, paying as much as $1,750 for an automatic rifle. Most NPA members are extremely poor, and $1,750 would be more money than many of them had ever seen. This gesture would also get the weapons out of the guerrilla army's hands. The government also offered defecting guerrillas an opportunity to enter an employment-training program.

But the communists were slow to respond. Many of them said they would voluntarily give up their rebellious ways as long as Aquino continued to live up to her words. Others retained their weapons and waited to see what Aquino would do in the matter of land reform. This is one area where more harm than good could be done trying to achieve social justice. As several of Aquino's economic advisers pointed out, it would not be especially beneficial to the Philippine economy to break up efficient farms and distribute them as small, unproductive parcels just to satisfy a vague promise of equity to all.

President Aquino herself said: "The problem is not so much to divide the land among the people but to let the people share more of the profits. By the way, there are no profits at the moment because of the sad state of the sugar industry. By dividing the land among the people one would only create more problems, because sugar production is not economically feasible on small plots. So what I have to do is break the sugar monopoly, revital-

A nun talks with communist rebels hiding in the mountains in Eastern Samar. The nun is trying to negotiate the surrender of NPA members to the new government of Corazon Aquino.

ize the industry, and get more workers participating in it. I plan to establish a model plantation for other sugar-plantation owners to copy."

What Aquino perhaps had in mind was the system used on Taiwan. In Taiwan, land reform had worked well because of long and careful planning. The new landowners were able to run highly productive farms even before they were given their parcels of land. Many of the new landowners in Taiwan were displaced Filipinos, and Aquino not only promised to investigate Taiwanese land distribution methods but also to try to lure back expatriate Filipino farmers and encourage them to establish this model system in the Philippines. She also named Ramon Mitra, described by knowledgeable observers as both an able politician and solid agricultural expert, as minister of agriculture.

The question was, however, would the 15,000 to 20,000 communist insurgents wait for such a long-range plan to take effect, or would they continue their guerrilla activities against the government and demand the immediate breakup of all the large plantations? By the spring of 1986 some of the communists said they were willing to talk about a cease-fire arrangement with the Aquino government, but few were willing to give up their weapons.

If the communist insurgency remained strong and persistent, Aquino's government would need a strong, revitalized army to combat it. Aquino named General Fidel Ramos as chief of staff to replace General Fabian Ver, who had fled into exile with Marcos. General Ramos is highly respected by the army and was, of course, one of the two top military men who had led the revolt against the ousted dictator. General Ramos' first move was to oust a number of elderly generals who had been Marcos favorites and replace them with competent young commanders who were respected by their own troops as well as by the U.S. Army officers who knew them. Ramos himself is a West Point graduate.

The next two problems President Aquino had to tackle involved setting up the form of government the Philippines would have in the future and attempting to retrieve the billions of dollars that Ferdinand and Imelda Marcos and their henchmen had apparently stolen from the Philippine people.

A NEW CONSTITUTION AND A SEARCH FOR THE MARCOS MILLIONS

To assure the future freedom of the Filipino people, President Aquino established a temporary provisional government with broad emergency powers to speed the dismantling of the dictatorial government she had inherited from Marcos. She also dissolved the 200-seat National Assembly and proposed the writing and adoption of a new constitution for the Republic of the Philippines. Her vice president, Salvador Laurel, was put in charge of the project.

Laurel said that the new constitution would take several months to write and then would be presented to the people for adoption or rejection at a national referendum. Aquino's provisional government probably would continue for some six months. The new constitution would be modeled after that of the United States and would include provisions for a president and two-house legislature. However, the president would be limited to a single six-year term and would be unable to declare martial law without the consent of the Congress.

Meanwhile, a full-scale effort was being made to discover just how much treasure the Marcoses had stolen from the Philippines, where the money was located, and how to get it back. At home there were new revelations almost daily concerning the sumptuous life-style of the exiled dictator and his wife while Marcos was in power.

The Filipino people had always had a vague idea of the regal splendor in which Ferdinand and Imelda Marcos had lived, but they did not really know just how grand this life-style was until they got their first close-up views of the interior of Malacañang Palace, the presidential residence.

President Aquino had said from the beginning that she would never live there because it was too ornate and pretentious to be the home of a president of a poor people. But she did promise to turn it into a public museum and ordered its doors opened to the general public. What the crowds who literally stormed inside saw was indeed shocking.

Rumors of Imelda Marcos' extravagance had often angered the people of the poverty-stricken Philippines. They had heard of her wild shopping sprees in the United States and Europe. Now they could see for themselves the hard evidence that proved these rumors to be true. She must have spent millions of dollars on jewels and jewelry alone, for numerous boxes were found filled with diamonds and other jewels as big as cherry tomatoes. In her boudoir was a gold wash basin. Nearby were quart bottles of French perfume and baskets full of imported soaps. In various closets were several thousand pairs of shoes, numerous shelves filled with expensive handbags, and more than a hundred clothes racks containing designer outfits. Dresser drawers were packed with thousands of dollars worth of fancy lingerie.

It was also apparent that Imelda and Ferdinand Marcos had thought of themselves as royal monarchs. Their bedroom intercoms in Malacañang Palace were labeled "King's Room" and "Queen's Room." Throughout the palace the walls were decorated with rare paintings appropriated from Manila's Metropolitan Museum, and the rooms were filled with priceless antiques.

In addition to the expensive decorations in Ferdinand Marcos' bedroom there was also clear evidence that the rumors about his poor health were true. Besides a hospital bed there was a kidney dialysis machine and related equipment as well as other professional equipment and medications. Two other dialysis machines were found in the palace.

The immediate question raised by Filipinos who visited the Malacañang Palace—many of whom earned less in a year than Imelda had spent on a pair of shoes—was, where did the Marcoses get the money to afford such opulence? President Marcos' salary had been just $5,700 a year.

The Filipino people were not the only ones asking this question. President Aquino and her aides not only asked it but began to make official inquiries into the sources of wealth that the Marcoses had accumulated. Jovito Salonga, head of Aquino's Presidential Commission on Good Government and a longtime critic of the Marcos government, estimated the Marcos assets at between $5 billion and $10 billion. Salonga was also charged with trying to recoup this fortune, which would at least partially pay off the country's national debt.

Documents Disclose Some of Marcos' Wealth

When they arrived in Hawaii the Marcoses and their party brought with them a planeload of baggage that included not only some of their personal belongings but also trunks containing more than a million dollars worth of newly minted pesos plus jewelry and bars of gold. In addition there were documents that disclosed real estate holdings as well as bank deposits in both the United States and Europe. Salonga said he had also found documents at Malacañang Palace that linked Marcos with bank deposits in Brazil, Switzerland, and the Bahamas.

Ferdinand Marcos made every effort to retain these documents, claiming they were his personal and private property, but the U.S. Congress and the Justice Department ruled otherwise. The United States, of course, was interested in the Marcos' holdings to see if they had been obtained illegally by the misappropriation of U.S. aid intended for use by the Philippine government for the Filipino people. The new Philippine government claimed that all of these holdings rightly belonged to the Filipino people and not to the Marcoses. There was little doubt that a long legal fight would ensue to determine just who did own these billions of dollars worth of treasure.

Among the immediate holdings revealed were millions

A back view of Malacañang Palace, overlooking the Passig River. The palace was once the summer villa of the rich Spanish grandees. It later became the residence of the Spanish governor general and then a residence of the presidents of the Philippines.

of dollars worth of real estate and office buildings in New York, Texas, and California. Other documents included bank passbooks and certificates of deposit worth millions more. It was further revealed that many of the Marcos millions were undoubtedly hidden in numbered, secret Swiss bank accounts, as Salonga had first indicated. Although ownership of these accounts is generally not revealed, the Swiss government announced that it would not withhold information on any funds in its banks that might be legally part of a foreign country's treasury. The Swiss government also froze all assets belonging to Marcos and his family.

The documents did not at first disclose any clear evidence of the misuse of foreign aid, but they did suggest that highly questionable "commissions" were paid to the Philippine government by some American companies for the right to do business in the Philippines. These commissions, or "kickbacks," could easily have been siphoned off by Marcos and his cronies for their own personal use. The U.S. Federal Corrupt Practices Act bars payment of commissions to obtain contracts from foreign governments.

All in all, these documents and other revelations plainly showed that the Marcoses made no distinction between the public treasury and their own private property.

How Marcos Got His Money

When Marcos first took office as president he declared that his personal assets amounted to only about $30,000. How he became a multimillionaire or even a billionaire during the next twenty years was one of the questions that investigators tried to answer in the weeks after he fled into exile. They uncovered some fascinating information.

For one thing, some seven tons of gold worth more than $75 million was reported to have disappeared from the Philippine treasury in recent years. The Philippines has long been a major gold producer. Up until 1978 much of this gold was refined in the United States and Great

Britain. But under martial law Marcos ordered that in the future all Philippine gold would be refined in the Philippines. Since this operation was controlled by the government's central bank, which was answerable only to Marcos, it would not have been difficult for Marcos and his cronies to get their hands on at least a part of these gold supplies.

Philippine teak and mahogany, both world-renowned commodities, were probably also sources of Marcos' apparently stolen wealth. Ernesto Maceda, Aquino's minister of natural resources, told investigators that some $960 million worth of teak and mahogany had been cut by Marcos' colleagues and smuggled out of the country between 1974 and 1980. "Marcos' cronies," Maceda said, "were the only ones who got the logging concessions, and their shipments were cleared for export on instructions from the top."

A continuing U.S. concern was what happened to the hundreds of millions of dollars that the Pentagon and State Department poured into the Philippines while Marcos was president. Although it would probably be months before a probe into possible abuses of U.S. economic and military assistance could be completed, the General Accounting Office (GAO) did issue a preliminary report stating that it could not account for at least $350 million in U.S. aid to the Philippines over the past several years. This figure was expected to grow.

Each day, week, and month seemed to bring new disclosures of allegedly stolen and hidden Marcos wealth. As Maceda said: "This was a government that raped its own country of its rich resources and directly robbed the nation's treasury to enrich just one man and his family and friends."

CAN STOLEN RICHES BE RECOVERED?

A major question being asked in both the Philippines and the United States was, could the allegedly stolen riches be recovered, and if so, how? The answer is, probably only partially, and that only through lengthy and painstaking investigation and legal action.

President Aquino herself wasted no time putting such legal efforts into motion, and in these efforts she was quietly backed by U.S. government officials. Whether or not Marcos himself could or would be prosecuted for his alleged thefts was a ticklish diplomatic matter. Aquino had revoked the passports of the Marcoses and their party as soon as they fled the Philippines, which technically meant they could flee no further than U.S. territory to avoid possible future prosecution. But the United States had offered Marcos sanctuary when he was considering going into exile, and it was doubtful that the State Department would permit his being driven out of such sanctuary to be prosecuted.

Nevertheless, as the investigations and disclosures continued, Marcos himself apparently began to fear being stripped of all his ill-gotten wealth and prosecuted by the new Philippine government and possibly the U.S. government. To avoid such an eventuality he began to look for someplace to live outside of U.S. territory where he could not be extradited. One of the places he considered was Panama, but the Panamanian government refused to allow him to move there.

Interestingly, some members of the Aquino government also began to make threats about reopening the investigation into the murder of President Aquino's husband, Benigno. After Marcos fled the Philippines, President Aquino said she would no longer attempt to prosecute the deposed leader for her husband's assassination and that the healing process should now begin in the Philippines. But various members of the newly created governmental Presidential Commission on Human Rights claimed that new evidence linking Marcos to the murder could not be ignored, and the investigation should be reopened and perhaps a new trial held even if it meant trying Marcos in absentia. What this new evidence was or whether President Aquino would change her mind about bringing Marcos to trial were not immediately made clear.

In fact, the long-range future of the Republic of the Philippines is not yet clear. There was little doubt that the conscientious, courageous, and highly dedicated new president of the Philippines, Corazon Aquino, would do her best to bring order out of the chaos into which her country had fallen. Whether or not her best would be good enough only the future can tell.

BIBLIOGRAPHY

Bain, David Howard. *Sitting in Darkness: Americans in the Philippines*. Boston: Houghton Mifflin, 1985.

Bocca, Geoffrey. *The Philippines: America's Forgotten Friends.* New York: Parents' Magazine Press, 1974.

Chaffee, F.H. *Area Handbook for the Philippines*. U.S. Government Printing Office, Washington, D.C., 1979.

Freidel, Frank. *The Splendid Little War.* Boston: Little, Brown, 1958.

Friend, Theodore. *Between Two Empires: The Ordeal of the Philippines, 1929–1946.* New Haven, CT: Yale University Press, 1965.

Grunder, G.A., and W.E. Livezey. *The Philippines and the United States*. Norman, OK: University of Oklahoma Press, 1951.

Kuhn, Delia and Ferdinand. *The Philippines: Yesterday and Today.* New York: Holt Rinehart, 1966.

Lawson, Don. *The United States in the Spanish-American War.* New York: Harper & Row/Abelard-Schuman, 1976.

______. *The United States in World War II*. New York: Harper & Row/Abelard-Schuman, 1964.

______. *Marcos and the Philippines.* New York: Franklin Watts, 1984.

MacArthur, Douglas. *Reminiscences*. New York: McGraw-Hill, 1964.

Paxton, John, ed. *The Statesman's Yearbook, 1984–85.* New York: St. Martin's Press, 1985.

Poole, Fred, and Max Vanzi. *Revolution in the Philippines: The United States in a Hall of Cracked Mirrors*. New York: McGraw-Hill, 1985.

Romulo, Carlos P. *I See the Philippines Rise.* New York: Doubleday, 1946.

Spence, Hartzell. *For Every Tear a Victory—The Story of Ferdinand E. Marcos*. New York: McGraw-Hill, 1964.

Steinberg, Rafael. *Return to the Philippines*. New York: Time-Life Books, 1980.

The World Almanac Book of Facts. New York: Newspaper Enterprise Association, 1986.

Wolfert, Ira. *American Guerrilla in the Philippines*. New York: Simon & Schuster, 1945.

INDEX

Illustrations are indicated by italicized page numbers.